The *Sams Teach Yourself in 24 Hours* Series

Sams Teach Yourself in 24 Hours books provide quick and easy answers in a proven step-by-step approach that works for you. In just 24 sessions of one hour or less, you will tackle every task you need to get the results you want. Let our experienced authors present the most accurate information to get you reliable answers—fast!

SAMS Teach Yourself Paint Shop Pro 5 in 24 Hours

This is called the Tool palette

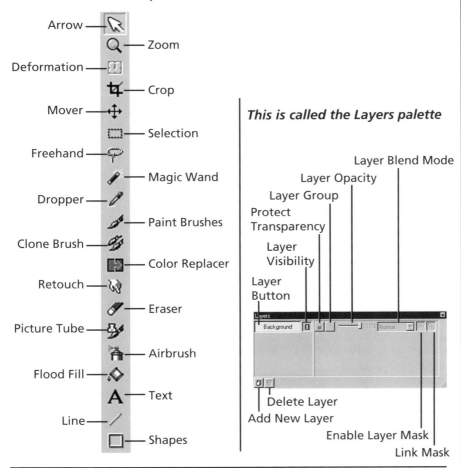

Arrow
Zoom
Deformation
Crop
Mover
Selection
Freehand
Magic Wand
Dropper
Paint Brushes
Clone Brush
Color Replacer
Retouch
Eraser
Picture Tube
Airbrush
Flood Fill
Text
Line
Shapes

This is called the Layers palette

Layer Blend Mode
Layer Opacity
Layer Group
Protect Transparency
Layer Visibility
Layer Button
Layers
Background
Delete Layer
Add New Layer
Enable Layer Mask
Link Mask

This is called the Toolbar

New
Save
Undo
Full Screen Preview
Copy
Normal Viewing
Toggle Control Palette
Toggle Layer Palette
Open
Print
Cut
Paste as New Image
Toggle Tool Palette
Toggle Color Palette
Toggle Histogram Window
Help

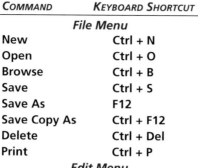

Paint Shop Pro Shortcuts

COMMAND	KEYBOARD SHORTCUT
File Menu	
New	Ctrl + N
Open	Ctrl + O
Browse	Ctrl + B
Save	Ctrl + S
Save As	F12
Save Copy As	Ctrl + F12
Delete	Ctrl + Del
Print	Ctrl + P
Edit Menu	
Undo	Ctrl + Z
Undo History	Shift + Ctrl + Z
Cut	Ctrl + X
Copy	Ctrl + C
Copy Merged	Shift + Ctrl + C
Paste As New Image	Ctrl + V
As New Layer	Ctrl + L
As New Selection	Ctrl + E
As Transparent Selection	Shift + Ctrl + E
Into Selection	Shift + Ctrl + L
Clear	Del
View Menu	
Full Screen Edit	Shift + A
Full Screen Preview	Shift + Ctrl + A
Normal Viewing	Ctrl + Alt + N
Image Information	Shift + I
Grid	Ctrl + Alt + G
Image Menu	
Flip	Ctrl + I
Mirror	Ctrl + M
Rotate	Ctrl + R
Crop to Selection	Shift + R
Resize	Shift + S
Color Menu	
Brightness/ Contrast	Shift + B
Gamma Correction	Shift + G
Highlight/ Midtone/ Shadow	Shift + M
Hue/Saturation /Luminance	Shift + H
Red/Green/Blue	Shift + U
Colorize	Shift + L
Posterize	Shift + Z
Edit Palette	Shift + P
Load Palette	Shift + O

COMMAND	KEYBOARD SHORTCUT
Layer Menu	
Select Current Layer	Ctrl + (layer #)
Selection Menu	
Select All	Ctrl + A
Select None	Ctrl + D
From Mask	Shift + Ctrl + S
Hide Selection Marquee	Shift + Ctrl + M
Invert	Shift + Ctrl + I
Promote Layer	Shift + Ctrl + P
Float	Ctrl + F
Defloat	Shift + Ctrl + F
Mask Menu	
Hide All	Shift + Y
Invert	Shift + K
Edit	Ctrl + K
View Mask	Ctrl + Alt + V
Capture Menu	
Start	Shift + C
Window Menu	
New Window	Shift + W
Duplicate	Shift + D
Fit to Window	Ctrl + W

BROWSER MENUS

COMMAND	KEYBOARD SHORTCUT
File Menu	
New Folder	Ctrl + B
Update Thumbnails	F5
View Menu	
Refresh Tree	Ctrl + F5
Find Menu	
File Name	Alt + F3
ImageFile Menu	
Delete	Ctrl + Del
Other	
Center Floating Tool Palettes	Shift + Ctrl + T
Hide/Restore All Floating Palettes	Tab
Hide/Restore Toolbar	T
Hide/Restore Histogram	H
Hide/Restore Layers Palette	L
Hide/Restore Tool Palette	P
Hide/Restore Controls Palette	O
Step Through Tools	Spacebar

T. Michael Clark

SAMS Teach Yourself

Paint Shop Pro 5

in 24 Hours

SAMS

A Division of Macmillan Computer Publishing
201 West 103rd St., Indianapolis, Indiana 46290 USA

Sams Teach Yourself Paint Shop Pro 5 in 24 Hours

Copyright © 1999 by Sams Publishing

International Standard Book Number: 0-672-31362-6

Library of Congress Catalog Card Number: 98-85493

Printed in the United States of America

First Printing: September 1998

00 99 98   4 3 2 1

Trademarks

Warning and Disclaimer

EXECUTIVE EDITOR
Beth Millett

ACQUISITIONS EDITORS
Laura Frey
Karen Whitehouse

DEVELOPMENT EDITOR
Kezia Endsley

MANAGING EDITOR
Patrick Kanouse

PROJECT EDITOR
Rebecca Mounts

COPY EDITORS
June Waldman
Carol Bowers

INDEXER
Kelly Talbot

PROOFREADER
Gene Redding

TECHNICAL EDITORS
Kelly Murdock
Laren Leonard

INTERIOR DESIGN
Gary Adair

COVER DESIGN
Aren Howell

LAYOUT TECHNICIANS
Michael Dietsch
Ayanna Lacey
Heather Hiatt Miller

Overview

Contents

Foreword

Access the Artist Inside

"I don't know much about art, but I know what I like." Sound familiar? Sure, we can all appreciate the beauty of Claude Monet's waterlilies or Ansel Adams' breathtaking land-scapes. But most of us probably feel the creation of images—Art—really belongs to a highly trained artistic elite. The rest of us should just be happy with a box of 64.

Wake up and smell the mouse! Art isn't just for artists anymore. The arrival of affordable personal computers and software has opened up a host of areas that used to belong to the "experts," such as typesetting, tax preparation, and creating and editing visual images. Now with the advent of digital imaging programs such as Paint Shop Pro, you don't need special training to make your own artistic vision come to life.

Making great solutions accessible to everyone is at the heart of what we do at Jasc Software. Our company was started in 1990 by Robert Voit, an airline pilot and computer enthusiast who passed the time between flight assignments writing game and database software for his friends. The first version of Paint Shop Pro appeared in 1992, when it was offered as shareware on electronic bulletin boards (ancestors of the web).

From these simple beginnings, we've grown into a company with nearly 100 employees worldwide. But we've stayed true to our roots. As the proud publisher of Paint Shop Pro, Jasc Software is still committed to making technology that's widely available, affordable, and easy to use. Unlike expensive, professional graphics programs that you need a life-time to master, we like to think of Paint Shop Pro as image and photo editing "for the rest of us."

That's why we're excited about this book, *Sams Teach Yourself Paint Shop Pro 5 in 24 Hours*. We believe this guide makes Paint Shop Pro, already one of the easiest image- and photo-editing programs around, even more accessible.

No matter what your level of experience, this book will help you get the most from your Paint Shop Pro. In a few short sessions, you'll be able to create eye-catching business and communications that get noticed; design great web site graphics; build handy digital photo archives for work or home; share photos electronically with family or friends; and much more.

I'm confident that *Sams Teach Yourself Paint Shop Pro 5 in 24 Hours* will open a whole new world of artistic possibilities for you. Get ready to access the artist inside!

Kris Tufto
Chief Executive Officer
Jasc Software, Inc.

About the Author

T. Michael Clark is the author of several prominent books on computer imaging software. Titles include *Sams Teach Yourself Photoshop 5 in 21 Days* and *Photoshop 5 Filters f/x and design* from Coriolis. Michael's first book, *Paint Shop Pro Web Techniques* from New Riders Publishing, was one of the first titles to showcase the growing powers of Paint Shop Pro.

With the advent of the World Wide Web, Michael is able to combine his many talents. An artist practically from birth, freelance photographer, computer consultant, certified programmer-analyst, and full-time author, Michael also owns and operates GrafX Design (`http://www.grafx-design.com`), a web site that offers online tutorials, product reviews, and a host of lessons on computer imaging topics. Michael is also an associate member of i/us, the site for visual professionals, and a regular contributor to Usenet graphics newsgroups. He is very glad to be able to share his love of the Internet with his many readers and devoted fans.

Dedication

This book is, as always, dedicated to my lovely wife, Pamela.

Acknowledgments

Firstly, a very special thanks goes to three amazing women at Macmillan Computer Publishing: Jennifer Eberhardt, Beth Millett, and Karen Whitehouse. I can't thank you guys enough for believing in this project as much as I did, and for pushing so hard to have it realized. Another special thank you goes to my agent, Margot Maley. I'm so glad you were there to listen to me rant some afternoons when I needed to let off a little steam.

I'd like to thank the team, both in-house and external, that helped make this book possible. A project of this size could not be completed without tons of talented people. Some of these people are Jennifer Eberhardt, Kezia Endsley, Laren Leonard, Kelly Murdock, and Laura Frey. There are many more whose names I don't even know, but want to thank anyway. To John Kane for giving me my first break and for being there when it all began.

The software companies:

First of all, I'd like to thank the great people at Jasc Software for creating such a cool program and for being involved with, and as excited about, the project as the rest of us.

Shayne Jolie, and the rest of the gang (very cool people), at Auto F/X.

Michael, Todd, Skip, and the others (a unique bunch) at AlienSkin.

Alexandre Clappier from RAYflect.

Dwight Jurling from Ulead.

Lloyd Burchill from Flaming Pear.

My models:

Marianne Dodelet and my niece, Zoë Alexandra.

I'd like to thank the wonderful McMullan family (Lynne, Tom, Madeleine, and Samantha) for extending their hospitality to Pam and me when we needed to get away from it all for a couple of days during this project. We consider their B&B in Ontario to be our home away from home.

Lastly, but certainly not least, you, the reader, and the people who visit my web site regularly. I depend on many of you, and the wonderful ideas and questions you send me via email, for many of the ideas that go into my books and online tutorials.

Tell Us What You Think!

As the reader of this book, *you* are our most important critic and commentator. We value your opinion and want to know what we're doing right, what we could do better, what areas you'd like to see us publish in, and any other words of wisdom you're willing to pass our way.

As the Executive Editor for the Web Graphics and Design team at Macmillan Computer Publishing, I welcome your comments. You can fax, email, or write me directly to let me know what you did or didn't like about this book—as well as what we can do to make our books stronger.

Please note that I cannot help you with technical problems related to the topic of this book, and that due to the high volume of mail I receive, I might not be able to reply to every message.

When you write, please be sure to include this book's title and author as well as your name and phone or fax number. I will carefully review your comments and share them with the author and editors who worked on the book.

Fax: 317-817-7070

Email: desktop_pub@mcp.com

Mail: Executive Editor
           Web Graphics and Design
           Macmillan Computer Publishing
           201 West 103rd Street
           Indianapolis, IN 46290 USA

Introduction

Years ago (many more than I care to think about), I got my first microcomputer. At that time, I was still drawing and painting using traditional media such as pencil, pen and ink, and watercolor. That very first evening, as I sought to learn as much as I could about the strange beast staring back at me from atop the coffee table, I realized that there was a lot of potential for these machines to help artists create images.

Today my dreams have been realized. Virtually anyone can, for the cost of an entry-level desktop computer and Paint Shop Pro, create amazing images. Processes as simple as creating navigational and decorative graphics for web pages, or as complex as photo manipulation and restoration, are now within the grasp of the average computer user.

Of course, some users require a little help to get up to speed. After all, as the hardware and software involved become more powerful, they may also become more complex to use. That's where this book comes into play.

Between the covers of this book, I intend to help you gain the knowledge you need to get you going as quickly as possible. I do so by presenting two dozen one-hour-long (or less) lessons. Each lesson covers a specific topic that helps you not only accomplish a certain task using Paint Shop Pro but also build your expertise and comfort level when it comes to creating and working with digital graphics.

Who This Book Is For

With the advent of the World Wide Web, many people have discovered a new interest in graphics. Perhaps they've decided to create a personal home page, to put their small business on the web and take a do-it-yourself approach, or, being the office computer "expert," they've suddenly found their job description changed to include "corporate webmaster."

Whatever the reason, it's a fact of life that a lot of people are discovering the power of digital graphics. With the price of computers, software, digital cameras, and scanners coming down constantly, it's not unusual for people to suddenly find themselves surrounded with the power to create digital art that was, until recently, available only to those with tens of thousands of dollars worth of equipment.

With this newly found power, though, you may also find yourself bewildered. You'll be faced with new terms, hardware and software compatibility issues, printing and scanning problems, digital color, and more.

If any of these problems have raised questions in your mind, this book is for you.

Getting Started

I've always been of the opinion that learning should be fun and that it should involve lots of hands-on experience. With that in mind, I like to write my books and my online tutorials in a way that makes the lessons fun and inviting. I try not to assume anything on behalf of the reader. Whether I'm discussing a topic as complex as anti-aliasing, or something as simple as creating a button for a web page, I include step-by-step descriptions and as many illustrations as I feel necessary for anyone to be able to get a handle on the concept.

I really like to teach, and it is my sincerest hope that you find this book as easy to follow as I intend it to be and that you find it as much fun to read as it was to write.

Now let's get started!

PART I

Getting Started in Paint Shop Pro

Hour

HOUR 1

Paint Shop Pro Basics

Welcome to Paint Shop Pro! This hour covers the following topics:

- An introduction to Paint Shop Pro
- Installation instructions
- An overview of the Paint Shop Pro interface
- An overview of new 5.0 features

Introduction to Paint Shop Pro

Wow!

That truly was the first comment out of my mouth when I ran the first beta copy of Paint Shop Pro 5. And I'm not the only one. I heard many people say the same thing the first time they ran the latest version of this powerful, yet affordable, imaging program.

Not long before version 4 came out, I started writing online tutorials covering Paint Shop Pro's various features. When version 4 came out, I thought that a good book might be well received (and I was right).

Now that version 5 has appeared, I believe there is an even bigger need for more help and that a good Paint Shop Pro book is a must. The copy you're holding in your hands is the result of that belief.

Version 5 of Paint Shop Pro truly moves this fine product to a much higher level. With this version come many new features and options, which represent new concepts. To use this latest version effectively, you, the reader and digital artist, must learn to use these new higher-level features.

Why do you, and others like you, use Paint Shop Pro? I believe that there are several reasons. Paint Shop Pro, even with its new list of high-end features, is relatively easy to use and carries a modest price tag. Many competing products can easily cost 8 to 10 times more.

Another attractive feature of Paint Shop Pro is its speed. Some users say that opening Paint Shop Pro and making a correction to an image is faster than working in some other imaging programs.

Personally, I like some of the features in Paint Shop Pro that you just don't find in other software (one of my favorites is the Hot Wax filter).

As you read this book and become more familiar with Paint Shop Pro, I'm sure that you'll find some reasons of your own that make your experience with this fun-to-use, powerful paint program a great one.

Installation Advice

 Before you get started with the installation and periodically thereafter, you should stop by the Jasc web site (http://www.jasc.com) to see whether Jasc has made any point releases available. *Point releases* are bug fixes and updates to the program. These updates are available free of charge to registered users. You should be able to download the program and install by following the instructions on the web site.

As with many of today's programs, Paint Shop Pro comes with a built-in installation program. This program should run automatically upon insertion of the CD-ROM. If the installation program doesn't run automatically, you can use Explorer to find the Setup.exe file and then double-click the Setup icon to bring up the installation window.

The installation program presents a graphical menu, which enables you to install Paint Shop Pro, and some pretty funky music.

1

Under most conditions, you should be able to choose the default settings. For example, Windows asks you to verify the folder that Paint Shop Pro should be installed to. Unless you have a specific reason for choosing another drive or folder, the default is a good choice. The default folder is normally c:\program files\Paint Shop Pro 5\.

If you're new to Paint Shop Pro, or you want to see the new features, you can choose to take a tour. The guided tour on the CD-ROM does a great job of introducing version 5.

After you install Paint Shop Pro, you're pretty much ready to go.

Overview of the Paint Shop Pro Interface

To run Paint Shop Pro for the first time, click the Windows 95 Start button and then choose Programs, Paint Shop Pro 5, Paint Shop Pro 5 to open the main Paint Shop Pro window (see Figure 1.1). You also can double-click the PSP icon to start the program.

FIGURE 1.1.

The Paint Shop Pro main window.

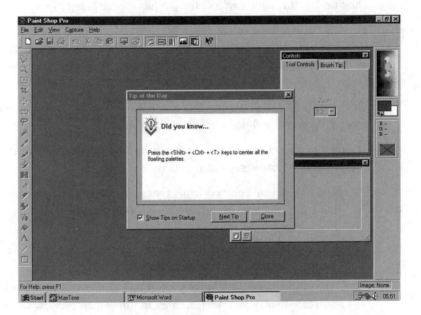

If you're a first time user, you'll notice how clean the interface is. If, on the other hand, you've used previous versions of Paint Shop Pro, you'll notice a few additions to the interface. If you've used or seen other graphics programs, you might also find yourself saying, "Wow!" The Paint Shop Pro interface is clean and easy to use; it's even customizable.

When you initially run Paint Shop Pro, and at the beginning of each subsequent use (unless you turn off the feature), you'll see a Tip of the Day dialog box (see Figure 1.2).

FIGURE 1.2.

The Tip of the Day dialog box.

Although you can turn off this feature, it's a useful way to pick up tips from the Paint Shop Pro team. To turn off the tips, remove the checkmark from the Show Tips on Startup checkbox. To restore this feature, simply run the Tip of the Day from the Help menu and place a checkmark in the Show Tips on Startup option.

The title bar, the menu bar, and the toolbar appear along the top of the main window.

The title bar is similar to any other Windows 95 program's title bar in that it contains a control icon and the standard Windows window control icons. These icons enable you to minimize, maximize, and restore the program's main window, as well as close the program.

The menu bar should be somewhat familiar. It contains a list of options that, when clicked, display a pull-down menu of suboptions.

The toolbar contains icons that are basically shortcuts to some of the common menu choices. The toolbar is separated into various palettes:

- The first palette contains icons for creating a new file, opening an existing file, saving a file, and printing a file. These options are the same as those found under the File menu choice.
- The second palette contains icons that enable you to quickly use four of the Edit menu commands: Undo, Cut, Copy, and Paste.
- The third palette contains two icons that enable you to control the display mode. You can display your image either in full-screen preview or in Normal Viewing mode.
- Along the left side of the screen, you have the Tool palette. It contains all of the tools you need to create and manipulate your images. I explain each tool in more detail in Hour 2, "Tools, Preferences, and Menus."
- Down the right side, you'll see the Color palette. The Color palette enables you to set the foreground and background colors (see Hour 2 for a demonstration).

- Floating in the upper-right corner of the main window, you'll see the Controls palette and the Layers palette.

  The Controls palette enables you to set the various options for a particular tool (see Hour 2 for a demonstration).

  The Layers palette enables you to work with layers, a powerful new feature in Paint Shop Pro 5. I cover the Layers palette briefly in Hour 2 and demonstrate, in depth, how layers work in Hour 11, "Layers."

At the bottom right of the main window, you have the status bar. It displays constantly updated information about the current image file. When you move the cursor over a tool, the status bar displays a short description of the tool's function. With the cursor over the current image, you'll see the cursor's x and y coordinates (this information is extremely helpful under certain circumstances as you'll see later), the current image's size in pixels and its color depth, and the current image's size in kilobytes.

Overview of New Features

Version 5 of Paint Shop Pro is amazing in its depth. Some of the new features were previously available only on programs costing hundreds of dollars more. Other new features are available only in Paint Shop Pro.

The following paragraphs briefly outline some of these new features; I go into more detail on how to access and use these features in later hours.

Direct Support for Kodak Digital Cameras

Paint Shop Pro 5 offers direct support for several models of Kodak digital cameras.

Normally, you would access digital cameras through the TWAIN interface, which you can still do, but you can now access the digital camera's interface directly from a menu choice in Paint Shop Pro.

Direct support enables Paint Shop Pro to take care of some of the interface details, such as which port the camera is plugged into.

With the camera plugged in and turned on, you can access any images stored in the camera and manipulate them in Paint Shop Pro.

Support for Graphic Tablets

With Paint Shop Pro 5, you now have support for pressure-sensitive graphic tablets such as Wacom's Art Pad.

Pressure-sensitive tablets enable you to draw and paint using a *stylus*, or pen, on a tablet. The tablet plugs into a serial port on your computer and gives you a more natural way to draw and paint your images.

Although you could use a tablet with previous versions, the pen acted much as a mouse would, and the pressure-sensitive options were not available.

With version 5, however, you can now use the pen and tablet in a more natural way, getting thicker or darker lines as you draw.

Tubes

Tubes are a really cool addition to Paint Shop Pro 5. They enable you to paint with predefined patterns. Paint Shop Pro includes a library of tubes, and hundreds more are available on the Internet.

Along with the huge, and growing, collection of tubes, you can also create your own. I demonstrate how to do so in Hour 14, "Picture Tubes."

Layers

Layers are, to me at least, the most exciting new feature in Paint Shop Pro 5. Layers enable you to do many things that you could not do without some difficulty (or maybe not at all) in previous versions.

Layers are analogous to sheets of tracing paper. You can have part of your image on one layer and another part on another layer. One difference between Paint Shop Pro layers and the tracing paper, though, is that in Paint Shop Pro you can make all the layers visible. You also can blend the information on different layers in many ways.

You can use layers to create incredible collages and montages, create easily editable web buttons, apply different textures to images with ease, blend images in ways you never thought possible, and much more.

I demonstrate layers and layering techniques in Hour 11. In addition, I use layers throughout this book so that you can see how valuable this new feature really is.

Using Online Help

As with many other Windows programs, Paint Shop Pro offers extensive online help. You can access the online Help feature from the menu bar. Choose Help, Help Topics to open the tabbed Paint Shop Pro Help window (see Figure 1.3) and the Help Topics: Paint Shop Pro Help dialog box (see Figure 1.4).

FIGURE 1.3.

The tabbed Paint Shop Pro Help window.

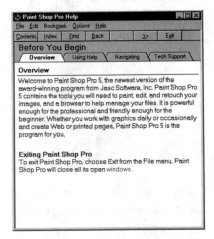

FIGURE 1.4.

The Contents tab of the Paint Shop Pro Help Topics dialog box.

The Help Contents window is arranged to facilitate browsing. You can choose a subject to display a list of subtopics. Choosing a subtopic brings up several paragraphs that explain the subtopic in detail in the tabbed Help window.

If you need to find a certain topic, you can click the Index tab (see Figure 1.5).

The Index tab displays the available topics alphabetically, and you can use either the cursor keys (on the keyboard, the up arrow or down arrow) or the mouse in the scroll box to scroll through the topics.

FIGURE 1.5.

The Index tab of the
Paint Shop Pro Help
dialog box.

Even better, though, you can type the subject that you're looking for and, as you type, the Help dialog box will hone in on the subject (assuming that the subject is actually available).

Whichever Help model you choose, you should find the online help very…well, helpful.

The Help files contain hotlinks (much like web pages) that show you more detail in the form of words or images that help you understand the topic you've chosen.

Taken altogether, the Help files are a great resource that you should spend some time exploring.

Summary

You have covered a lot of ground already. You learned how to install Paint Shop Pro, explored its interface (maybe for the first time), and glanced at the new features available in version 5. In Hour 2 you learn more about the plethora of tools and preferences available to you in Paint Shop Pro.

Workshop

The workshop contains a question and answer section to help answer the most commonly asked questions and quiz questions to help you solidify your understanding of the material covered.

Q&A

Q How do I get a copy of the latest version of Paint Shop Pro?

A You can order it directly from the Jasc web site at `http://www.jasc.com`.

Q How do I determine which installation method is best for my needs?

A The Typical installation is well suited for most people. Unless you're very familiar with computers, I recommend using that installation method. The Custom method enables you to pick and choose which components to install, but if you're not familiar with the program and with computers in general, you should probably stick with the Typical install.

Q How do I determine which version of Paint Shop Pro I'm using?

A Choose Help, About Paint Shop Pro. The version number is displayed in the splash screen.

Quiz

1. Name one method for starting Paint Shop Pro.
2. How do you turn off the Tip of the Day dialog box?
3. Can you use a pressure-sensitive graphics tablet with Paint Shop Pro?
4. Can you use TWAIN hardware with Paint Shop Pro?

Answers

1. You can double-click on the PSP icon on the desktop to start Paint Shop Pro.
2. To turn off the Tip of the Day, remove the checkmark from the Show Tips on Startup check box.
3. Yes, Paint Shop Pro 5 supports pressure-sensitive tablets. You can set the preferences under File, Preferences, General Program Preferences. Select the Cursors and Tablets tab and set the tablet preferences to the way that you work.
4. Yes, you can use TWAIN scanners and digital cameras with Paint Shop Pro. If you own a Kodak digital camera, you'll find that it's directly supported as well.

HOUR 2

Tools, Preferences, and Menus

This hour introduces the following tools and menus:

- The toolbar
- The toolbox and its options and tools
- The various palettes
- The various menus
- The various preferences you can set to customize Paint Shop Pro

The Toolbar

The toolbar holds some of the most frequently accessed menu choices (see Figure 2.1).

FIGURE 2.1.

The Paint Shop Pro toolbar.

Having these popular menu choices available as icons means that often-used menu choices are one click away. For example, the first icon in the toolbar enables you to open a new image. Clicking the New icon (it looks like a small rectangle with one corner folded over) saves you from choosing File, New. The other icons represent Open (File, Open); Save (File, Save); and Print (File, Print).

These four icons represent the four most common File menu choices. The next four icons represent the most common Edit menu choices: Undo (Edit, Undo); Cut (Edit, Cut); Copy (Edit, Copy); and Paste (Edit, Paste).

Sequentially, the next two icons on the toolbar are the Full Screen Preview and the Normal Viewing Preview icons. Clicking the Full Screen Preview icon displays the active image against a full-screen black background. You can choose this option from the Toolbar icon or from the View menu. To return to normal viewing, click the Full Screen Preview screen.

The Normal Viewing icon returns an image with a reduced or enlarged zoom factor to normal (1:1) magnification.

The next portion of the toolbar holds five icons that toggle the various palettes on and off. From the left, you have the following icons:

- The Tool Palette icon. (This palette is on by default.) Note that this tool resembles the Zoom tool but is actually a small wrench. The Tool Palette icon toggles the Tool palette on and off.

- The Controls Palette icon. (This palette is on by default.) The Controls Palette icon toggles the Controls palette on and off.

- The Color Palette icon. (This palette is on by default.) You can toggle the Color palette on and off by clicking this icon.

- The Histogram Palette icon. (This palette is off by default.) This icon toggles the Histogram palette on and off.

- The Layers Palette icon. (This palette is on by default.) The Layers Palette icon toggles the Layers palette on and off.

Being able to toggle palettes on and off is very helpful, especially if you run Paint Shop Pro on a lower-resolution screen or in a smaller window.

If you generally don't need immediate access to a certain palette, you can toggle it off. If you suddenly find that you're in need of something within that palette, though, you can simply toggle it back on.

On the far right is one last icon—the Help icon.

Selecting the Help icon won't, as you might expect, bring up the online help. Rather, selecting this icon changes the regular mouse cursor by adding a question mark to it. That's when the magic starts. You can move this new cursor over virtually any part of the Paint Shop Pro window and click the mouse. Doing so brings up the help window, but the help text is about whatever you clicked on. For example, if you click the Help icon and then click the Color palette, the Help menu in Figure 2.2 opens. This feature is called *context-sensitive* help.

FIGURE 2.2.

Context-sensitive help.

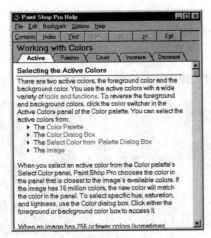

Point-and-click help is great if you suddenly need help, know what you need help with, but can't remember the name of the tool or palette.

The Toolbox

The toolbox contains, quite naturally, the Paint Shop Pro tools (see Figure 2.3).

FIGURE 2.3.

Paint Shop Pro's Tool palette.

You have tools to make selections, draw and paint, create lines and shapes, and more. As you move the mouse over the tools in the toolbox, Paint Shop Pro displays a small tag telling you what the tool is.

Even better than just seeing the tool's name, though, you also find a description of what the tool does. This brief information appears in the lower left of the status bar. To see how this feature works, hold the mouse over the Zoom tool (see Figure 2.4).

FIGURE 2.4.

The Zoom tool.

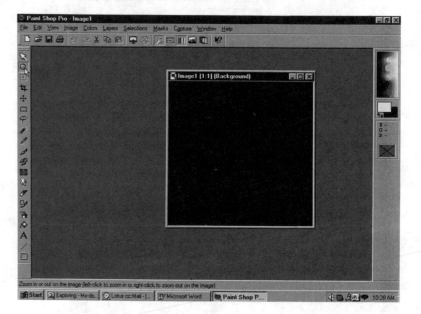

You should see a small tag displaying the tool's name (Zoom) just below your cursor. As well, you should be able to read the tool's description—Zoom in or out on the image (left-click to zoom in or right-click to zoom out). Small tags identify each tool in the toolbox, and each has a short description in the status bar. The following sections describe the tools that are available in Paint Shop Pro.

The Arrow Tool

The Arrow tool enables you to quickly bring an image to the front. This technique is helpful when you have several images open at one time. Simply select this tool and click on the image you want to bring to the front.

The Arrow tool does double duty. It also enables you to scroll around images that are too big to be completely displayed in their window. To scroll around an image, simply click-and-drag with the Arrow tool (the cursor icon becomes a hand icon during this procedure) to move the image around within its window.

The Zoom Tool

The Zoom tool enables you to zoom in on an image for close-up, detailed work, and it also enables you to zoom out to see the entire image at once. Left-clicking on the current image zooms in; right-clicking on the current image zooms out. (Hold the Zoom tool and click over the image area that you want centered while increasing or decreasing the zoom factor.)

The Deform Tool

The Deform tool enables you to rotate, resize, skew, or distort the current layer. (This tool is inactive on the Background layer.) With a multilayered image, you can use this tool to quickly rotate, resize, skew, or distort the contents on any layer other than the Background.

When you select the Deform tool, a bounding box surrounds the object(s) on the current layer. This bounding box has several control handles: one at each corner of the box; one in the middle of each side, the top, and the bottom; and one in the middle. The control handles enable you to "deform" the object surrounded by the bounding box. You can, for example, resize and rotate the object(s). I describe this process in more depth in Hour 6, "Working with Deformations."

The Crop Tool

The Crop tool enables you to quickly crop an image. To do so, select the Crop tool and simply click-and-drag to outline the area you want to crop.

If you're not satisfied with the sizing or placement of the cropped area, don't worry. You can easily resize the cropping area by clicking-and-dragging the edges of the area, and you can click-and-drag the cropped area until it fits exactly over the portion of the image you want to crop. Once the cropping area is suitably placed and sized, simply double-click anywhere within the image to finalize the cropping.

If you've taken a step that you're not happy with, you can always undo it by choosing Edit, Undo. In fact, you can undo several steps. Knowing that nothing's really permanent frees you to put a little playfulness into your explorations. Much can be learned by clicking away with some abandon. However, the best way to experiment is to work on backup copies. If you have only one copy of an image and you do make some irreversible change, you're out of luck. If, however, you work on a backup copy, nothing you do in Paint Shop Pro can damage the original.

The Mover Tool

The Mover tool performs a little magic. It moves whatever you place the cursor over no matter which layer is currently active. That is, the Mover tool knows which layer an object is on. If you have a green square on layer 1 and a red circle on layer 2, you can move either by simply selecting the Mover tool and clicking-and-dragging the object you want to move.

For this tool to perform its magic, though, each object must be on its own layer because the Mover tool can't differentiate different objects on the same layer. It will move the entire layer that's associated with the object you click-and-drag. Still, this tool is very useful for placing multiple objects over several layers.

The Selection Tool

The Selection tool enables you to make selections. You can select rectangular, square, elliptical, and circular areas of an image for easier manipulation. Before you can cut, copy, and paste portions of an image, you must select that portion. Selections also enable you to work on the selected area of an image without affecting the rest of the image.

To select a portion of the current image, simply click the Selection tool. Hold the Selection tool cursor over the active image and click-and-drag to define an area of the image. You can set the various selection shapes in the Controls palette, which I describe later in the section on palettes.

The Freehand Tool

The Freehand tool enables you to draw freehand selections anywhere on the current image.

You can make three types of selections with the Freehand tool. You can simply draw a freehand selection, you can draw a point-to-point, or polygonal, selection, and you can draw a Smart Edge selection.

- The Freehand option enables you to draw selections of any shape. All you need to do is click-and-drag the mouse to define the area you want to select.
- The Point-to-Point option enables you to make polygonal selections. All you need to do is click at each corner of the polygon as you move the mouse. When you're done, simply double-click to finish the polygonal selection.
- The Smart Edge option attempts to define your selection based on brightness and contrast between adjacent pixels. You can use this option to loosely draw around an area, and the Smart Edge will try to draw the best selection around the area.

The Magic Wand Tool

The Magic Wand tool enables you to select an area of your image based on its color. You simply select this tool and click within an area. All pixels of the same color and adjacent to the pixel under the cursor are selected, as if by magic. You can set some rules and a tolerance that will help this tool perform its magic. These options can be set in the Controls palette.

The Dropper Tool

The Dropper tool enables you to pick up colors from the current image. You can use this tool to set both the foreground and the background colors.

To set the foreground color, simply select the Dropper tool and left-click over a color in the current image. To set the background color, do the same but right-click instead.

This tool enables you to set the foreground and background colors from colors currently in use in an image.

The Paint Brushes

The Paint Brushes tool enables you to paint on your images. You can use the Controls palette to select different brushes and to set the opacity, the hardness, and the size and shape of the brushes. From the Controls palette, you can also select a texture that enables you to imitate painting over various surfaces.

The Clone Brush

The Clone Brush tool enables you to copy portions of an image over other areas of the same image or any other open image. This tool can selectively remove or edit parts of an image. For example, you can use this tool to remove electrical lines from an otherwise pristine scenic photograph.

The Color Replacer

The Color Replacer tool enables you to selectively change one particular color into another throughout the entire image. The process for swapping color seems mysterious, yet it is fairly simple.

To swap an existing color with a new color throughout an image, set the foreground color to the color you want to change and set the background color to the color you want to change to. To do so, use the Dropper tool or click on the foreground/background color swatches to display the Color dialog box.

With the colors set, select the Color Replacer tool and double-right-click anywhere in the image to swap any existence of the foreground color with the current background color.

You can swap any pixel with the existing background color in the image with the current foreground color by double-left-clicking anywhere in the image.

I describe this process again with some examples you can work through in Hour 4, "Creating Your First Image."

The Retouch Tool

With the Retouch tool, you can selectively retouch areas of your images. The Retouch tool uses the same brush tips as the other painting and drawing tools, but the controls enable you to lighten, darken, soften, change the saturation, and more. Select this tool to make minor retouches to a photograph.

The Eraser Tool

The Eraser tool enables you to erase portions of your image. You can erase to the current background color or, on higher layers, to transparent. The Eraser tool uses the same brush tips as the drawing and painting tools.

The Picture Tube

The Picture Tube tool, new to version 5, enables you to paint on an image using tubes. Tubes are built from images arranged in a grid. These images, which usually share a common theme, display at random as you paint with the Tube brush.

This concept is easier to explain through example than with words, and I cover tubes in more depth in Hour 14, "Picture Tubes."

The Airbrush

The Airbrush tool simulates an airbrush. Changing the opacity and density settings changes the amount of digital paint that is sprayed onto your image.

The Flood Fill Tool

2

The Flood Fill tool fills an image or a selected area of your image with either the current foreground or the current background color. Left-clicking fills with the foreground color, and right-clicking fills with the background color.

You can also choose to fill the area, or the entire image, with a pattern or with a gradient. You can use any image as a pattern for the fill.

The gradients go from the current foreground to the current background colors, and you can choose from several patterns. You can use gradients to give depth to an image, build complex masks, and create special effects. Examples appear throughout the book.

The Text Tool

The Text tool creates and enters text onto your images. The text can be in any font. The Text tool is quite easy to use. Simply select it and click somewhere within your image to bring up the Text Tool dialog box. You can select the size, the font, and several other options. This dialog box is where you enter the text you want to appear in your image, as well. You have many opportunities to use the Text tool as you work through this book.

The Line Tool

The Line tool enables you to draw lines on your images. You can set the width, choose whether the line will be anti-aliased, and draw either normal lines or Bézier curves.

Anti-aliasing is a process that softens the hard edges in digital graphics. The process uses mathematics and involves using varying shades of colors between the contrasting edges. This process produces a smoother, softer-looking image. You'll see how anti-aliasing affects different images throughout the rest of the book.

Bézier curves are curves named after the mathematician who developed the algorithm, or set of computer steps, that enables graphic artists to draw and manipulate smooth curves on the computer.

The Shapes Tool

Last, but not least, the Shapes tool enables you to draw outlined or filled shapes such as rectangles, squares, ellipses, and circles.

Although the preceding descriptions of the tools were brief, as you work through the following chapters, you'll get plenty of hands-on experience with the various tools.

The Menus

The various menu choices are available from the main menu bar. Several of the main choices will be familiar to you as a Windows user. The File, Edit, Windows, and Help choices are similar to those same choices available in most Windows programs. However, they may hold some unfamiliar choices.

As well, many main menu choices in Paint Shop Pro may be unfamiliar. You may not recognize choices such as Image, Layers, Selections, and Masks if you are new to digital imaging. These menu choices will rapidly become second nature, though, as you work your way through this book.

The Menu Choices

When you first open Paint Shop Pro and you haven't yet opened an image file, the following menu items are available: File, Edit, View, Capture, and Help.

Upon opening a file or creating a new file, the following choices are added: Image, Colors, Layers, Selections, Masks, and Windows.

Each main menu choice offers subtopics. Choosing one of these subtopics may lead to another submenu or a dialog box that enables you to set the options for a particular choice.

Any menu choice followed by a small triangular arrow leads to additional related subtopics. Any item followed by an ellipsis opens a dialog box. Any other menu choice performs an action.

Under the File menu, for example, the first grouping contains the following choices: New..., Open..., Browse..., and Close. The ellipses after the first three items mean that these selections open a dialog box in which you must enter information so that the option can carry out its task. The fourth choice, Close, is not associated with any symbols. Therefore, the Close option simply performs an action (it closes the current file) without the need for any additional information.

The following sections briefly outline the menu choices; you'll get some hands-on experience with the various choices as you work through the book.

2

The File Menu

The File menu enables you to open, close, create, save, import, export, browse, print, and batch convert image files. As you work through the rest of the book, you'll become quite proficient at using the File menu options.

One other choice under the File menu is Preferences, which I explain later in this chapter.

The Edit Menu

The Edit menu enables you to Undo the most recent change, access the Undo History (multiple undo), Cut, Copy, Copy Merged, Paste, Clear, and Empty edits.

Most of these choices will be familiar to you if you've used other Windows-based programs. A couple that might be unfamiliar are the Clear and Empty choices:

- Clear deletes anything in a selected area of your image. The selected area will delete to transparent if on a higher layer and will delete to the current background color if on the background layer. Although similar to cutting, the Clear option does not copy the selected area to the Clipboard. You have an opportunity to use the Clear option later in the book.

- Empty enables you to free up some computer memory. You can choose to empty either the Clipboard or the Undo History. If you have many files open and find that the system is running out of memory, you can get a little back by emptying the Clipboard and the Undo History.

The View Menu

The View menu gives you access to different viewing modes. You can view the image and the workspace in Full Screen Edit mode. This mode is toggled, meaning that you can choose it from the View menu to select it and choose it once again to deselect it. The Full Screen Edit mode opens the Paint Shop Pro window to completely cover any other open windows. As well, this mode hides the menu bar. You can still access the menu bar by pressing and releasing the Alt key, though.

The next view is Full Screen Preview mode. In this mode, all that you see on the screen is your image. To return to Normal Viewing mode, press the Esc key or click anywhere on the screen.

You can use other menu choices in the View menu drop-down box to zoom in and zoom out, access information about the current image, and enter creator information.

Finally, you can use the View menu choice to access the Grid, the Rulers, and the Toolbars dialog box. I'll demonstrate the grids and rulers in several exercises throughout the book.

The Image Menu

The Image menu enables you to change and manipulate your images by flipping, mirroring, and rotating them. From this menu, you can also choose the various plug-in filters. Paint Shop Pro comes with several filters that enable you to create different effects.

You also can purchase many third-party filter programs. After installing the extra filters, you can access them through the Image, Plug-in Filters menu choice. I demonstrate how to install and set up filters in Hour 15, "Applying Filters."

The Colors Menu

The Colors menu is where you can access all the color options pertaining to your images. You can adjust the color, colorize, change the brightness and contrast, select a palette, set a color for transparency, and set the number of colors in your image.

As you work through the rest of this book, you use the choices under the Colors menu quite often—often enough that many of the choices and their options will become second nature.

The Layers Menu

From the Layers menu you can add, duplicate, delete, rearrange the order of, and change the properties of the various layers that make up your image.

I demonstrate and cover layers in detail in Hour 11, "Layers." Many of the exercises throughout the book give you plenty of opportunity to use and become accustomed to layers.

The Selections Menu

The Selections menu enables you to manipulate selections. For example, you can create selections, modify the current selection, save and load selections, and create masks from your selections.

I demonstrate selections throughout the book, specifically in Hour 5, "Creating and Working with Selections."

The Masks Menu

The Masks menu gives you access to the masking functions. You can create, edit, save, and load masks. I cover masks in detail on Hour 12, "Masks."

The Capture Menu

You can use the Capture menu to make screen captures of your images (such as for use on the web). Under the Capture menu, you can set up the various preferences for which key combinations will run the Screen Capture function, whether it will capture the whole screen or just a portion of it, whether the cursor will be included in the capture, and so on.

The Windows Menu

The options on the Windows menu will be familiar to you if you've used Microsoft Windows for any length of time. This menu is pretty much standard across all Windows programs. The choices under this menu enable you to set the way that windows are displayed within Paint Shop Pro.

The Help Menu

The Help menu enables you to use online help, which was discussed earlier in this chapter. You can search for keywords and get context-sensitive help from the help menu choices.

Using the Palettes

Palettes are common in graphics programs. They operate like visual menus and let you set options for various tools. Paint Shop Pro has four palettes you can use to set options and choose tools and color settings. They are as follows:

- The Color palette
- The Control palette
- The Layer palette
- The Tool palette

You can turn the palettes on and off via the View, Toolbars command. Choose View, Toolbars to open the Toolbars dialog box (see Figure 2.5).

FIGURE 2.5.

The Toolbars dialog box.

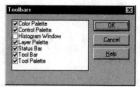

To turn off a palette, simply remove the checkmark next to its entry in the dialog box. To restore a palette, place a checkmark next to its entry.

The four palettes enable you to use the various settings and options associated with the palette.

The Color Palette

The Color palette enables you to set the foreground and background colors for the drawing and painting tools (see Figure 2.6).

FIGURE 2.6.

The Color palette.

You can set a color by moving the mouse over the main swatch in the Color palette. Clicking the left mouse button sets the foreground color, and clicking the right mouse button sets the background color.

You can open the Color dialog box by clicking on either the foreground or background color swatch (see Figure 2.7).

The Controls Palette

The Controls palette enables you to set the options associated with a particular tool (see Figure 2.8).

FIGURE 2.7.

The Color dialog box.

FIGURE 2.8.

The Controls palette showing the Tool Controls tab for the Zoom tool.

Figure 2.9 shows the options you can set for the Paint Brushes tool Brush Tip.

FIGURE 2.9.

The Controls palette showing the Brush Tip options for the Paint Brushes tool.

The Layers Palette

The Layers palette enables you to set the options and blending modes for the layers that make up your images (see Figure 2.10).

You can also create new layers and delete layers from within the Layers palette by using the two small icons at the bottom left of the palette. The first enables you to create a new layer, and the second enables you to delete a layer.

FIGURE 2.10.

The Layers palette.

You can create/delete layers by clicking on these two icons. You can also drag-and-drop layers on either icon. Dragging-and-dropping a layer onto the New Layer icon duplicates the layer, and dragging-and-dropping a layer onto the small trashcan deletes the layer.

The Tool Palette

The Tool palette contains the various tools that you can use to paint, draw, make selections, and so on. The tools in this palette were discussed previously in this chapter.

Setting Preferences

Like many of today's advanced programs, Paint Shop Pro enables you to set various preferences. To set Paint Shop Pro's preferences, choose File, Preferences. Another pull-down menu opens, with the choices you see in Figure 2.11.

FIGURE 2.11.

The Preferences sub-menu.

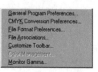

Each of the menu choices in this pull-down menu opens a dialog box in which you can set some preferences to make using Paint Shop Pro easier for you.

General Program Preferences

You can tab through the Paint Shop Pro Preferences dialog box to set up levels of undo (higher levels take more memory), the size and color of rulers, how cursors display (precise or tool shape), and more (see Figure 2.12).

CMYK Conversion Preferences

The CMYK Conversion Preferences dialog box enables you to tell Paint Shop Pro how to handle conversions between CMYK (a standard file mode for high-end printing) and RGB files (the standard mode for onscreen computer images) (see Figure 2.13).

FIGURE 2.12.

The Paint Shop Pro Preferences dialog box.

FIGURE 2.13.

The CMYK Conversion Preferences dialog box.

Unless you plan to send your images to a prepress shop (something you might want to do to print 5,000 full-color brochures), you really don't need to bother with this setting.

File Format Preferences

The File Preferences dialog box enables you to set the default image size for new files (File, New) and to set the preferences for the raw data (RAW) and Windows Meta-File (WMF) file formats (see Figure 2.14).

FIGURE 2.14.

The File Preferences dialog box.

File Associations

The Associations dialog box enables you to set and unset the file formats to associate with Paint Shop Pro (see Figure 2.15). Any file whose file format is associated with Paint Shop Pro opens in Paint Shop Pro when you double-click on its icon.

FIGURE 2.15.

*The Associations dia-
log box.*

This feature is handy if you always want to, for example, edit JPG or GIF files with Paint Shop Pro. With their respective file formats set in the Associations dialog box, you can open JPG and GIF files in Paint Shop Pro by double-clicking their icons in Explorer.

Customize Toolbar Preferences

The Customize Toolbar dialog box enables you to select which tools are displayed and thus made available through the toolbar (see Figure 2.16).

FIGURE 2.16.

*The Customize Toolbar
dialog box.*

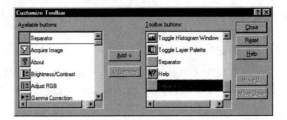

You could, for example, add a button to acquire images with your scanner. This option would save you from having to go through the various menu choices to select the acquire option.

After you become more comfortable with Paint Shop Pro, you should take the time to see which buttons are available. Setting up a couple of buttons for often-used features can be a real timesaver.

Color Management Preferences

If you own Windows 98 or NT 5, you can take advantage of the built-in color management of these operating systems.

Monitor Gamma Adjustments

The Monitor Gamma Adjustment dialog box enables you to set the Gamma (overall color cast and brightness/contrast) of your monitor (see Figure 2.17).

FIGURE 2.17.

The Monitor Gamma Adjustment dialog box.

2

To brighten the display, move the sliders to the right. To darken it, move them to the left. If your monitor gives a color cast (that is, the neutral gray seems to contain a little red, green, or blue), you can adjust each color separately. To do so, unlink the channels and move the sliders separately until the color cast disappears.

If you're not sure how your display is set, you should ignore the settings in this dialog box and leave the defaults. You can't harm your monitor by playing with these settings, but they are best left alone if you think that your monitor is functioning correctly.

Summary

In this hour, you learned how to find your way around Paint Shop Pro. You should spend a little extra time exploring the interface and familiarizing yourself with the different tools and menus.

Workshop

The workshop contains a question and answer section to help answer the most commonly asked questions and quiz questions to help you solidify your understanding of the material covered.

Q&A

Q If I forget which tool I need for a certain job, how do I go about finding the tool I need?

A You can select the Help icon. When you do so, the cursor becomes a small question mark with a pointer. You can then click on any tool to get a brief description of its function.

Q Why are some menu choices also offered as icons?

A It's probably because different people like to work in different ways. For example, I prefer to keep my hand on the mouse and rarely use the shortcut keys. I actually work more quickly this way, whereas others may work more efficiently with the keyboard shortcuts.

Q Can I change the way the interface looks? Can I, for example, change the icons?

A Yes, you can change which tool icons are used, and you can select from several different icons to enhance Paint Shop Pro for the way that you work.

Q Where can I set the options for any given tool?

A You can usually set a tool's options in the Controls palette. You can open the Controls palette by clicking the Controls Palette icon on the toolbar or by choosing View, Toolbars and placing a checkmark next to the Controls Palette checkbox.

Quiz

1. If you wanted to pick up a color from an image and copy that color to another image, which tool would you use?

2. Is it possible to change one color in an image into another color? How?

3. Is it possible to work on an image without the clutter of all the tools and palettes getting in the way? How?

4. How do you switch between normal view and full-screen viewing modes?

Answers

1. You should use the Dropper tool.

2. Yes. You can do so with the Color Replacer tool.

3. Yes. You can toggle the screen between Full Screen Edit mode and normal mode. You can also selectively turn on and off the various palettes and toolbars.

4. You can switch the editing modes by pressing Shift+A. Doing so will toggle between the two editing modes.

Hour 3

Opening, Saving, and Printing Files

This hour introduces the following actions in Paint Shop Pro:

- Opening a file
- Saving files
- Importing and exporting files
- The basics to printing files

Opening a File

To get an image into Paint Shop Pro, you can use one of the following techniques: create a new image (File, New), open an existing image (File, Open), or import an image (File, Import) from a digital camera or scanner.

Opening a New File

To open a new file, choose File, New. Doing so opens the New Image dialog box (see Figure 3.1).

FIGURE 3.1.

The New Image dialog box.

Within the New Image dialog box, you can set the width, height, and resolution of the new image. You can set the background color and the image type (number of colors used for the new image). You'll be accessing this dialog box many, many times as you work through the rest of this book.

Generally, I give you the dimensions, resolution, color, and image type. Later, as you create your own images, you can decide on the settings that are appropriate for your own images.

Opening an Existing File

You can open an existing file by choosing File, Open. This action opens the standard Windows Open dialog box (see Figure 3.2).

FIGURE 3.2.

The Open dialog box.

Browsing for an Existing File

You can browse through folders to find the file or you can enter a file's name. You can also see previews of the files if they're recognized by Paint Shop Pro.

You can use Paint Shop Pro's file browser (see Figure 3.3) to browse through folders visually.

FIGURE 3.3.

The Browse dialog box.

The file browser enables you to see, at a glance, all of the images in a folder. A small button, or *thumbnail*, represents each image in the currently selected folder.

To open an image after identifying it from its thumbnail, simply double-click on the thumbnail. After you successfully open an image, you can manipulate it in many different ways. You learn about the amazing things that you can do with new and existing images as you progress through this book.

Importing Files

You can import images into Paint Shop Pro from any digitizing hardware—a scanner or a digital camera, for example.

Paint Shop Pro offers an interface to your TWAIN hardware. When you buy a scanner or a digital camera, you must install it. Part of the installation process involves installing the drivers and the device's software.

Figure 3.4 shows Paint Shop Pro importing a photo by running Hewlett-Packard's DeskScan II 2.7.

If you have a TWAIN scanner or digital camera, the interface you see will depend on the software included with your hardware.

FIGURE 3.4.

Paint Shop Pro running the TWAIN scanner driver for a Hewlett-Packard desktop scanner.

Although the process of importing an image is a little more complicated than simply opening a file, this step is much like accessing an image from your hard drive.

Saving Files

After you acquire your image, correct it, or manipulate it to your satisfaction, you need to save it to your hard drive.

Starting with version 5, Paint Shop Pro has its own file format. If you created new layers during the processing of your image, you should use Paint Shop Pro's native format, .psp, to save the file. This format preserves the layers and their associated blending modes. Saving under any other format with the exception of the .psd file format (Photoshop's native format) discards any separate layer information and *flattens* the image into one layer.

Flattening the image is not a bad thing and is actually necessary for formats such as JPG and GIF. If you've done extensive work with layers, though, you may want to save at least two copies of your image. One copy should be in PSP format and the other can be in some other format, GIF for a web-based file, for example.

Another factor to consider is saving the image as you work. You might want to create a temporary working directory and save incremental backups of your work. Even with the advanced state of today's technology, computers crash. They most often do so right after you've put in several hours of uninterrupted work and just before you finally decide that you should save the changes you've labored over.

You can save every 5 to 10 minutes or so and use names such as Image001, Image002, and so on. When you are finished, you can save the final image (most likely as a PSP file) and delete the Image files from your temporary folder.

Aside from the Save option, you can use Save As or Save a Copy. These two options are essentially the same, except Save a Copy doesn't affect the current image in any way.

For example, using Save As to save your image to the GIF format flattens the image and reduces the color palette to only 256 colors or fewer. Using Save a Copy saves a copy of the image with the layers flattened and the color palette reduced but leaves the current image in its unaltered state.

Exporting Files

In addition to saving your images, you can export them. Exporting your images requires the use of export filters. Paint Shop Pro comes with one built-in export filter. In fact, exporting is how (at least in part) you create tubes. I demonstrate how to create tubes in Hour 14, "Picture Tubes."

> Exporting a file is similar to saving a file. The main difference is that exporting a file enables you to use certain export filters or plug-ins. Export filters or plug-ins allow third-party programmers to extend the built-in capabilities of a program such as Paint Shop Pro.

In addition to the built-in export filters, many third-party filters are available. You can get filters that, for example, hide a copyright number in your image to help you keep track of your digital artwork.

Printing Basics

After all the work you put into your masterpiece, you may want to print it. Paint Shop Pro makes printing relatively easy. The first thing you should do is choose File, Page Setup. Doing so will bring up the Page Setup dialog box (see Figure 3.5).

FIGURE 3.5.

Page Setup dialog box.

Within this dialog box, you can set the size and source of the paper. For most printers, the default settings, Letter 8.50×11.0 inches and Auto Feeder, should be fine.

You can also set the Orientation option to either Portrait (vertical orientation) or Landscape (horizontal orientation). You can choose to center the image on the page and to set the left and top margins. Using the Scale option, you can set the size of the image.

You can also specify the Print Output setting. If you own a color inkjet, you can select the Color option, or you can select Greyscale if you own a black-and-white printer (for example, a laser printer). You can even print a CMYK separation.

To preview the job before sending it to the printer, select File, Print Preview to open the Print Preview screen (see Figure 3.6).

FIGURE 3.6.

You can preview an image before you print.

This screen gives you an idea of what your printed image will look like. It is a good idea to preview your image if only to make sure the margins are set where they should be.

If you're satisfied with the preview, you can click the Print button. This step opens the dialog box specific to your printer and enables you to print the image. It's as simple as that!

Summary

In this hour you've learned how to open, save, import, export, and print your images. You might want to practice opening some images (you can find a few nice images on the Paint Shop Pro CD-ROM) and saving them as different file types. You might even want to open a file and print it to see how images look on your printer.

In the next hour I show you how to create your first image. I discuss some of the concepts you should know about before starting an image, and I take you on a brief tour of the various tools that are available in Paint Shop Pro.

3

Workshop

The workshop contains a question and answer section to help answer the most commonly asked questions and quiz questions to help you solidify your understanding of the material covered.

Q&A

Q How do I know what my image will look like when it's printed?

A You can preview your printed image by choosing File, Print Preview.

Q What types of files can Paint Shop open and save?

A Paint Shop Pro directly supports 46 different file types, including the most popular image types. A few of these are BMP, JPG, GIF, TIF, and PSD (Photoshop files).

Q Why would I want to export a file?

A Exporting files enables you to use export filters or plug-ins that extend the capabilities of Paint Shop Pro.

Q What is the purpose of the PSP file extension?

A Having multiple layers in a file is a new feature in version 5, and the PSP file type (native Paint Shop Pro file) enables you to preserve the layering information. I discuss layers in Hour 11, "Layers."

Quiz

1. How do you save a Paint Shop Pro file for use on the web?

2. Is it important to preview your image before printing it?

3. Is it possible to view a folder of files visually and, if so, how?

4. Are there any built-in export filters in Paint Shop Pro?

Answers

1. You need to save the file as a GIF or a JPG. You can do so via the Save As or the Save a Copy choice under the File menu.

2. It takes only a moment to preview your image before printing it. It might be a good idea to do so until you're familiar with the printing process.

3. You can view all of the image files in a folder that are compatible with Paint Shop Pro by choosing File, Browse.

4. Yes, Paint Shop Pro comes with the Tube Export filter. This filter enables you to create tubes (see Hour 14).

HOUR 4

Creating Your First Image

This hour introduces the following topics regarding images:

- Issues to consider before constructing your first image
- Creating your first image
- Editing your first image
- Fixing mistakes in an image

Issues to Consider Before Constructing an Image

It's often quite tempting to just jump right in and start painting and drawing when creating a new image. However, stopping for a moment and thinking about the image before you actually begin can end up saving you time.

Some of the things to consider are the overall size of the image, including its dimensions, the number of colors needed (which can affect the resulting file size), and the file size, especially if the image is intended for the web.

Choosing an Image Size

Whether the image is intended for the web, general onscreen viewing, or print media, the dimensions are one of the first things to consider.

If your image is intended for onscreen presentation, you'll usually want it to fit within the limits of a computer screen.

More and more people use 800×600 settings for their computer monitors. Some are even using much higher resolutions. Nevertheless, many people still run their screens at 640×480. If you know your audience well or are designing for a particular screen resolution, you're all set. If not, choose the resolution of your own screen or smaller.

With that decision out of the way, it's time to decide on the resolution in terms of dots per inch (dpi) or pixels per inch (ppi). If you're designing for onscreen or web use, set the resolution to 72dpi, which is the norm for most computer screens. The differences you'll encounter won't be significant and, for onscreen use, the most important aspect to consider is width and height anyway.

If you'll be printing your image, or having it printed, the dpi you choose becomes a more important issue. If your final output is destined for print, you'll want to use a much higher resolution than that used for onscreen presentations.

Most of today's printers are capable of 300×300, 600×600, or higher resolution, and sending a 72dpi image to one of these printers will result in either a much smaller image than you wanted or final print quality that's just not acceptable.

Be aware, though, that images with a higher resolution require much more memory. An image at 72dpi that's 4"×6" (which is about the standard size for prints you get back from most one-hour photo stores) is about 385KB uncompressed, whereas the same image at 300dpi takes up a whopping 6MB of hard drive space.

Keep in mind, too, that resizing an image down results in better quality than resizing an image up. What I mean is that if you take a small image and make it larger, you'll be disappointed with the results. If you take a larger image and resize it down, though, the results, although not perfect, will be much better.

Choosing an Image Type

Another issue to consider is the *image type*, or number of colors (color resolution). If you're scanning an image into Paint Shop Pro, you should normally use the highest setting available—especially for real-world images such as photographs. You should use a lower color setting when scanning in black-and-white art, though. If you're opening and working on an existing image, plan to stay with the existing color resolution.

Normally, your scanning software will adjust the number of colors based on the type of image its scanning. You can still use a higher number of colors, especially if you'll be applying effects to the image.

When you are finished working on the image, you can lower the number of colors if necessary. This change decreases the final file size and may even be necessary if you are saving to a file type such as GIF.

When starting a new image, you are faced with the most options as far as color resolution is concerned. This is when you have to decide on the image type. The image type you choose depends on the image you are creating and its intended purpose (such as final output method).

Generally, you should start out with a high color resolution, especially if you intend to use any of the special effects in Paint Shop Pro. Most of the effects are greyed-out, or not available, when you work on lower color resolution images.

You can always change the image type after you complete the image. This step is, in fact, necessary if you're working on an image with thousands or millions of colors that needs to be converted to a GIF file for the web.

4

I recommend keeping a copy of the original image in the higher color resolution in case you need to make changes later. This approach means that you won't have to change the color resolution over and over, which ultimately causes an image's quality to degrade.

The choice for image type, or number of colors in an image, is made when you open a new image. Figure 4.1 shows the New Image dialog box.

FIGURE 4.1.

The New Image dialog box.

This dialog box pops up when you choose File, New. You can set the width, height, and resolution. You can also set the background color and the image type. For image type, you can choose from the following options:

- 2 (1 bit)
- 16 (4 bit)
- Greyscale (8 bit)
- 256 (8 bit)
- 16.7 million colors (24 bit)

You can also reset the color resolution by choosing either Colors, Decrease Color Depth or Colors, Increase Color Depth. The Decrease Color Depth menu gives you more control than you get from the New File dialog box and the Increase Color Depth menu choice. From the Decrease Color Depth menu, you can also choose 32,000 colors; 64,000 colors; or an arbitrary number of colors for any image.

Normally, I start an image with 16.7 million colors so that I can effectively apply all the tools at my disposal. The image can always be downgraded to a lower color resolution when I'm done. That said, let's open a new image and explore a few of the tools at hand.

Creating a Simple Image

The best way to learn is to roll up your sleeves and get right to it. The following exercise introduces the Paint Shop Pro tools used for drawing, painting, and creating lines and shapes.

Using the Shapes Tool

To get started, open a new image at 500×500 pixels with the resolution set to 72ppi, the background set to white, and the image type set to 16.7 million colors. Then follow these steps:

1. Set the foreground color to one of your favorite colors by moving the mouse over the Color palette and clicking the color.
2. Select the Shapes tool from the Tool palette.
3. In the Controls palette, set the shape to Rectangle, the style to Outline, and the outline width to 2.
4. Click-and-drag the mouse somewhere within the image window. As you drag the mouse, a rectangle forms, grows, and changes shape. When you finally release the mouse, a perfect rectangle will be drawn where the outline was.

Try another!

1. Reset the foreground color by choosing a color from the color swatch in the Color palette.

2. In the Controls palette, change the style to Filled and draw another rectangle. This one will be filled with the foreground color instead of just outlined in it.

3. Choose another color and, in the Controls palette, set the shape to Circle.

4. Click-and-drag the mouse in the image window again. This time you'll be drawing a circle. You may notice that, unlike the rectangular shape, the circle is drawn from the center out. This piece of information will come in handy when you want to draw more complex shapes by combining various lower-level shapes.

Avoiding Aliased Images

If you haven't placed a checkmark in the Antialias checkbox of the Controls palette, and if your circle is large enough and it contrasts enough in color with the background, you may notice that it's a bit jagged (see Figure 4.2).

FIGURE 4.2.

Aliased circle.

4

This jaggedness is called *aliasing,* and it's the result of taking an analog shape, such as a circle, and digitizing it. A shape like a circle is *analog* by nature in that it has an infinite number of points that make up its circumference.

When you draw a circle on a computer screen, it must be represented by pixels. All of these pixels together make up a grid of 640×480 pixels, 800×600 pixels, 1,024×768 pixels, and so on. Because the circle is being drawn on a grid, it is digitized. That is, only a certain number of points are available, and each point on the circumference of the circle that is being drawn must be represented by one of the pixels that make up the grid on your computer screen.

What all of this really means to you, the digital artist, is that many of your shapes and lines will be aliased. This, of course, means that your images will have jagged edges. Or does it? Actually, it does and it doesn't. How can that be, you ask? Simple! You can use a process known as *anti-aliasing* to gives your jagged edges the appearance of being smooth.

Anti-aliasing uses mathematics and shades of colors that range between the colors along the edges to fool your eye into believing that the edge is smooth

Figure 4.3 shows another filled circle drawn in Paint Shop Pro. This time, when I drew the circle, I placed a checkmark in the Antialias checkbox in the Controls palette.

FIGURE 4.3.

Anti-aliased circle.

To show you the difference, I zoomed in on both Figure 4.2 (the aliased circle) and Figure 4.3 (the anti-aliased circle). Seeing the two images side by side will give you a better idea of what aliasing and anti-aliasing are all about (see Figure 4.4).

The image containing the aliased circle is obviously made up solely of black and white pixels, whereas the image containing the anti-aliased circle shows pixels of varying shades of gray along the circle's edge. It's these pixels that give the second circle its appearance of smoothness.

In version 5 of Paint Shop Pro, most of the tools have anti-aliasing capabilities. I go into more detail on drawing shapes in Hour 7, "Drawing Tools and Techniques."

FIGURE 4.4.

Aliased and anti-aliased circles side by side.

Using Brush Tips

Close the image you've been doodling on and open a new image with the same settings as before. (You can save the first one if it is the beginning of a masterpiece you want to get back to later.) Then follow these steps:

1. Select the Paint Brushes tool. In the Controls palette, click the Brush Tip tab to bring up the Brush Tip palette (see Figure 4.5).

FIGURE 4.5.

The Brush Tip palette.

2. You can use the controls in the Brush Tip palette to set the various options for the Paint Brush tool. You can set the size, the opacity, the hardness, the density, and the step of the brush. Also, you can select a brush from the pull-down menu. To access this menu, click the Brush icon at the upper-right of the palette.

   You can choose from a variety of brushes. I talk more about brushes in Hour 8, "Painting Tools and Techniques."

4

3. Select a brush, play with the settings, and draw on the new image to get the feel for the various brushes and their settings. Change the color, the brush type, and the opacity to see what happens.

One nice option here is the brush preview in the upper-left corner of the Brush Tip palette. This small window shows you what the brush looks like and gives you a good idea of the effect you'll get when you use any given brush.

4. Try lowering the opacity. If you lower the opacity enough, you'll be able to see previous lines you've made through the new lines you're drawing. This powerful feature enables you to mimic real-world drawing tools.

Figure 4.6 shows how I mimicked a yellow highlighter marker drawn over some black text.

FIGURE 4.6.

Yellow highlighter over black text.

To create this quick highlighter fakery, I simply added black text to a new image and then drew over the text with a yellow brush. I set the brush to Normal with the shape set to Round, and I set the size to 104 (just enough to cover the height of the text).

I set the opacity to 52. (I played around with this setting a couple of times and used Edit Undo until I got just the opacity effect I wanted.) I set the hardness to 0 (I wanted a very soft edge so that it would blend into the white background just as an older marker might do). I left the density set to 100 and the step set to 25. All of these settings combined to give the effect I wanted, that of a marker highlighting text.

Try playing around with the brushes and their settings to see how they work. Don't worry if some of the options seem confusing for now. I cover them in depth in Hour 8.

Editing a Simple Image

Paint Shop Pro also enables you to edit existing images. You can use the drawing and painting tools as well as the Text, the Line, and the Shape tools to change an image.

Two other tools that enable you to edit an existing image are the Color Replacer tool and the Retouch tool. The Retouch tool acts much the same as the Paint Brushes tool, and, in fact, you can set the different options for this tool as if it were a brush.

The difference is that you can use the Retouch tool to apply various retouching effects such as lighten, darken, soften, emboss, and more. I cover these options in more depth in Hour 17, "Retouching Your Images."

The Color Replacer tool, although powerful, can be somewhat confusing. I think, though, that if you follow along with the next example, the workings of this tool will become clear.

To see how the Color Replacer tool works, open a new 500×500 image with a white background and with the image type set to 16.7 million colors. Then follow these steps:

1. Set the foreground color to black. Make sure that it's black; it must have the value 0 for each of the colors Red, Green, and Blue. You can see these numbers scroll as you move over the color swatch in the Color palette.

2. You should be able to move the mouse far enough to the left of the color swatch to get the color to be perfectly black. If you can't quite get it, just click on the foreground color swatch to bring up the Color dialog box (see Figure 4.7).

FIGURE 4.7.

Color dialog box.

3. With the Color dialog box open, you can easily enter the RGB values. After you enter zeros for each entry, click OK and the foreground color will be perfectly black.

4. Draw two circles that don't touch. You can place them in opposite corners as I've done in Figure 4.8.

FIGURE 4.8.

Two circles filled with black.

5. Change the foreground color to a really dark blue. You don't have to be too fussy, just make sure that the color is almost black. The values for the color I'm using are R: 4, G: 4, and B: 8.

6. With the new foreground color set, draw a fill rectangle so that it partly covers each circle.

FIGURE 4.9.

Two circles filled with black and a nearly black rectangle.

7. Select the Color Replacer tool.

8. Click the Tool Controls tab in the Controls palette and set the Tolerance to 0.

9. Set the background color to a nice bright yellow. You don't need to be fussy; just select a color that's different from the two circles and the rectangle. You can set the background color by right-clicking a color in the main color swatch in the Color palette.

10. With the new background color set and the foreground color still set to the color you chose for the rectangle, double right-click anywhere in the image.

     What happened? The rectangle should have turned yellow. It turned yellow because that's the current background color. The Color Replacer tool replaced all the pixels containing the current foreground color with the current background color.

11. You can reverse the process by double left-clicking. Try it. Double left-clicking replaces the color of all pixels with the current background color with the current foreground color.

12. With the image back to its original state, bump the Tolerance up to around 50.

     Double right-clicking replaces the color of all three objects with the current background color.

The Tolerance setting controls how close a color needs to be to the color being changed before it gets replaced with the new color. Almost like magic, right? And now you know how it works.

I encourage you to play with this awesome tool until you feel comfortable with it.

Fixing Errors

To help you keep your creativity alive, Paint Shop Pro has an Undo feature (a multiple Undo feature, actually). If you make a change, or several changes, to an image and find that you don't like the changes or that they aren't quite what you expected, you can undo them.

To undo the most recent change, choose Edit, Undo. This step backs up to just before the most recent change you made. To see Undo in action, open a new file and draw a shape. Then follow these steps:

1. Select another tool such as the Line tool or the Paint Brushes tool and draw over the shape you created.

2. Choose Edit, Undo, and the line or the mark you made will disappear.

3. Choose Edit, Undo again, and the shape disappears, as well.

4. Oops! What if you intended to keep the first shape? No problem! Choose Edit, Redo to make the shape reappear.

There's even an Undo History. If you choose Edit, Undo History, you'll get the Undo
History dialog box (see Figure 4.10).

FIGURE 4.10.

*The Undo History dia-
log box.*

In Figure 4.10 the Undo History dialog box contains a list of the most recent changes I
made to the image, which is also visible in the figure. To restore an earlier image, simply
click the corresponding point in the Undo History dialog box.

You may want to upgrade to version 5.01 if have version 5.00. This upgrade
fixes a couple of problems and adds several new options such as the Edit,
Redo that undoes the previous Edit, Undo.

Unfortunately, the history is linear, so you can't pick and choose which Undos you want
to use. Anything else that is highlighted in the list is also undone. This feature is a great
way to return to a specific point in your work, though.

Summary

In this hour, you've learned a little about how to create an image, draw shapes, and use
the Paint Brush tools. You've also learned how to edit an image and how to change any
color in the image to another color. As well, you've seen how to undo an error and redo
the undo, and you've taken a quick look at the Undo History feature.

The next hour explains how to create, edit, save, and load selections.

Workshop

The workshop contains a question and answer section to help answer the most commonly asked questions and quiz questions to help you solidify your understanding of the material covered.

Q&A

Q How do I set the size of a brush?

A You can change a brush's size and some of its other characteristics in the Controls palette.

Q How can I draw an outline of a shape such as a circle or a square?

A You can set the Shapes tool to draw either filled or outlined shapes. These options can be set in the Controls palette.

Q I drew a shape in a color other than the color I really wanted. What can I do?

A Choose Edit, Undo and redraw the shape after changing the color.

Q Can I undo a couple of steps?

A Yes, you can undo many steps that you've made. The default number is three, but you can change this setting in the Preferences dialog box. To set the number higher (you'll need more memory for this, though) or lower, open the Preferences dialog box (choose File, Preferences, General Program Preferences) and click the Undo tab.

Quiz

1. What guidelines do you use to pick your image size?
2. What is the easiest way to avoid aliased images?
3. Why should you open new images at 16.7 million colors?
4. Is it possible to change one color for another throughout an image?

Answers

1. The suggested size of the image really depends on what the image will be used for. For web images, file size is a little more important than the actual dimensions. I like to make an image large enough to be readily evident.

2. Make sure that the anti-alias option is checked on all the tools that you use to create an image.

3. Many tools and options require all available colors to work properly. You can always change the number of colors after you've completed the image.

4. Yes, you can change one color for another with the Color Replacer tool.

PART II
Editing Your Images

Hour

HOUR 5

Creating and Working with Selections

This hour introduces the following issues regarding working with selections:

- Using the selection tools
- Editing selections
- Loading and saving selections
- Learning about alpha channels

A *selection* masks off an area of an image so that you can make changes to that area without affecting the rest of the image. You can fill selections, run effects on them, and more. You can save selections and load them later. You can also copy and paste selections within an image or from one image to another, and you can add to and subtract from selections.

Using the Selection Tools

Selections are essential for creating and manipulating digital images, and Paint Shop Pro provides a number of tools for making selections. From the Tool palette, you can select one of three selection tools:

- The Selection tool
- The Freehand tool
- The Magic Wand tool

Each of these tools is discussed in the following sections.

The Selection Tool

The Selection tool enables you to make selections using different shapes. After choosing the Selection tool, you can set the desired shape in the Controls palette. You can choose from a rectangle, a square, an ellipse, and a circle. Using the Selection tool is similar to using the Shapes tool.

To try out the Selection tool, open a new 500×500 image at 72dpi with the background set to white and then follow these steps:

1. Select the Selection tool.
2. In the Controls palette, set the shape to Rectangle. For the moment, ignore the Feather value and the Antialias checkbox.
3. Place the mouse cursor in the upper-left corner of the image and click-and-drag toward the lower-right corner of the image.
4. As you drag the mouse, you'll see an outline of a rectangle. When you release the mouse, however, the rectangle becomes a marquee (see Figure 5.1). Some people refer to this marquee as "marching ants" because of the movement.
5. To clear the selection, either choose Selection, Select None or click anywhere outside of the marquee area.

Try making a couple of selections using the other shapes. If you forget to remove one selection before making another, the first selection disappears. Later in this hour you see how you can keep any current selection and either add to it or subtract from it. You also learn how to modify the selection.

The Freehand Tool

The second selection tool is the Freehand tool. You can use the Freehand tool to draw freehand selections. To see how this tool works, clear any other selections you still have active by choosing Selections, Select None. Select the Freehand tool and click-and-drag with it around the image as if you were drawing a doodle.

As you draw, you'll see a line being drawn by the tool. When you release the mouse button, the line turns into a marquee and a straight line joins the starting and ending points (see Figure 5.2).

FIGURE 5.1.

A rectangular selection.

FIGURE 5.2.

A freehand selection.

The Freehand tool has several settings available from the Controls palette, as well. You can draw freehand as you did in the previous example. You can also draw point-to-point or Smart Edge selections.

Point to point enables you to draw polygonal selections. To do so, select the Freehand tool and set the Selection Type option to Point to Point in the Controls palette.

5

Move the mouse cursor into the image and click somewhere. Move the mouse again and click once more. As you continue to move and click, you'll see lines being drawn between the points where you click. To finish the selection, simply double-click. What you should end up with is a polygonal selection (see Figure 5.3).

FIGURE 5.3.

A polygonal selection.

The third option for the Freehand tool is using the Smart Edge. With the Smart Edge option, you can get Paint Shop Pro to help you make difficult selections along edges of contrasting areas. To see how this option works, clear any current selections you have by choosing Selections, Select None. Then follow these steps:

1. Select the Shapes tool and set the Style to Filled in the Controls palette. Draw a circle in the upper-right corner of the image. Change the shape to a rectangle and draw a rectangle below and to the right of the circle (see Figure 5.4).

   If you're not sure how to complete these steps, refer to Hour 4, "Creating Your First Image."

2. With the shapes drawn, select the Freehand tool and set the Selection Type option to Smart Edge in the Controls palette.

3. Move the mouse cursor to a point along the bottom left of the circle.

4. Click-and-drag the mouse toward the rectangle. As you drag, you'll see a bounding box (see Figure 5.5). When you get to the point where you're just overlapping the rectangle, as shown in Figure 5.5, release the mouse button.

FIGURE 5.4.

A circle and a rectangle drawn with the Shapes tool.

FIGURE 5.5.

A bounding box highlights the edge that the Smart Edge is selecting.

5

5. Click the mouse again without moving it and then move the mouse to the lower-left corner of the rectangle.

6. Double-click the mouse; you should end up with a selection like the one in Figure 5.6.

Although this powerful tool is a little difficult to work with at first, it is worth learning. The Smart Edge option of the Freehand tool enables you to make selections around areas that might otherwise be impossible.

FIGURE 5.6.

A completed selection along the lower left of the circle and the rectangle drawn with the Smart Edge Freehand tool.

The Magic Wand Tool

You can use the Magic Wand tool to select areas of an image based on the RGB value, hue, or brightness. You can set the Tolerance level to select more or fewer pixels based on the relative values. The Magic Wand tool is quite easy to use. You simply select it, set the options, and click on a portion of the image that you want selected.

To try this tool, open a new 500×500 image at 72dpi with the background set to white and then follow these steps:

1. Draw a filled rectangle in one color (I used a pale blue) and a filled circle in another, very different, color (I used red).

2. Make the shapes overlap, as shown in Figure 5.7.

3. Select the Magic Wand tool.

4. In the Controls palette, set the Match Mode option to RGB and the Tolerance option to 15.

5. Click somewhere on the circle. The circle should be outlined by a selection marquee. The marquee means that the circle has been selected. Nothing else has been selected, though—only the circle.

Only the circle is selected because it is red, the rectangle is blue, and the background is white. If the overlapping rectangle were a shade of red that closely matched the red of the circle and the tolerance was high enough, the rectangle would have been selected also.

FIGURE 5.7.

A circle and a rectangle drawn with the Shapes tool.

The Magic Wand tool doesn't care about the shapes of the areas it's selecting; it bases its selections on the Match Mode and the Tolerance settings.

 You may have noticed a Sample Merged checkbox in the Controls palette for some of the selection tools. When checked, this option allows selections to be made throughout all the layers of an image. I describe layers in depth in Hour 11, "Layers."

You can also make and adjust selections using the Selections menu. From the Selections menu you can

- Select All (Ctrl+A), which selects the entire image.
- Select None (Ctrl+D), which deselects the current selection.
- From Mask (Shift+Ctrl+S), which makes a selection based on the current mask. (Masks are covered in Hour 12, "Masks.")
- Invert (Shift+Ctrl+I), which inverts the selection. In other words, if you still have the circle selected from the previous section and you choose Selections, Invert, everything but the circle is selected. If you choose Selections, Invert again, the circle is reselected. Try it!
- Matting, which can remove fringes that sometimes appear around a selected area.
- Modify, which can modify a selection. (I cover this in more depth in the next section.)

- Hide Marquee (Shift+Ctrl+M), which hides the marquee (or marching ants) while leaving the selection active.
- Convert to Seamless Pattern, which can create seamless tiles for repeating patterns and backgrounds.
- Promote to Layer (Shift+Ctrl+P), which turns a selection into a new layer.
- Load from Disk, which loads a saved selection from your disk drive.
- Load from Alpha Channel, which loads a selection that you saved as a channel.
- Save to Disk, which saves a selection on your hard drive.
- Save to Alpha Channel, which saves a selection in an alpha channel.
- Float (Ctrl+F), which floats the selection and enables you to move the selected area around the image while leaving the area below untouched. In other words, you create a duplicate of the selected area, which you can freely move around within the image.
- Defloat (Shift+Ctrl+F), which drops the selected area. You can still move a selected area when you defloat it, but the actual area moves, not the duplicated area. You can, of course, float the selection again.

I explore some of these options in the next section and use most of these tools extensively throughout the remainder of the book.

Editing Selections

Making a selection is not necessarily the end of your work. You can add to the selection, subtract from the selection, expand and contract the selection, and more.

Adding to a Selection

After making an initial selection, you can add to it. To see how this option works, open a new 500×500, 72dpi image with the background set to white. Then follow these steps:

1. Select the Selection tool and, in the Controls palette, set the Selection Type to Rectangle.
2. Draw a rectangular selection in the upper-left corner of the image.
3. Place the mouse in the lower-right corner of your selection—not too near the corner, though. While holding down the Shift key, draw another rectangular selection.

   You should now have an area selected that resembles two overlapping rectangles (see Figure 5.8). Interesting.
4. Try that again, but this time, change the Selection Type to Circle and start somewhere near where the two rectangles overlap.

FIGURE 5.8.

Adding to a selection.

Hmmm…you should now have a fairly complex shape building up, consisting of a couple of rectangles and a circle (see Figure 5.9).

FIGURE 5.9.

Adding more to a selection.

5

You may be getting the idea that you can actually create some fairly complex shapes using just the selection tools, and you'd be right. In addition to adding to a selection, you can also subtract from it, as discussed in the next section.

Subtracting from a Selection

To subtract from a selection, select a selection tool and, while holding down the Ctrl key, make a selection that overlaps the current selected area. To give it a try, follow these steps:

1. Select the Selection tool and, in the Controls palette, set the Selection Type to Ellipse.

2. On the selection made in the previous section, move the mouse to the middle of the left side of the bottom rectangle.

3. Hold down the Ctrl key and draw an elliptical selection. When you release the mouse button, the ellipse will be cut from the selected area (see Figure 5.10).

FIGURE 5.10.

Subtracting from a selection.

Wow! Can you see some of the possibilities? You can use any of the selection tools to add to and subtract from a selection. Using these tools together, you can make very sophisticated selections. These selections can be around existing portions of an image or, as you've just done, made on new images.

To see how these techniques can be used, I subtracted a couple more shapes, filled the image with black, embossed it, and added a new layer in which I filled the selection with a wood texture. The result is shown in Figure 5.11.

All of these techniques are covered throughout this book. In fact, by the end of this book, you'll be able to create interfaces just like the one pictured in Figure 5.11.

Figure 5.11.

Creating a template for an interface from selections.

Expanding and Contracting a Selection

Sometimes a selection is almost right, but not quite the way you want it. You may need to expand or contract the selection. To do so, choose Selections, Modify, Expand or Contract and then enter a value in the dialog box. This step expands or contracts the selection by the number of pixels you entered in the dialog box.

Growing a Selection

At other times, you may need to include a little more of an area that has similarly colored pixels. You can do so by choosing Selections, Modify, Grow. This option is useful if you made a selection with the Magic Wand tool and, with the setting you chose for the Tolerance, selected most of the area you needed. Instead of resetting the Tolerance and trying again, Selections, Grow is often enough to get those extra pixels.

Selecting Similar Areas

Growing a selection grabs adjoining pixels, but what if the area you want isn't up against the area you've already selected? Simple. You can select areas in the image based on whether or not they are similar to the area already selected.

Say you have some black text on a white background and you select the background area by clicking on the background with the Magic Wand tool. Doing so selects the background area around the text, but it doesn't select any white areas inside letters such as *O* and *P*.

5

No problem. Choose Selections, Modify, Select Similar. This sequence selects the rest of the white areas (because the background that you selected is white), including those pesky areas inside of certain letters.

Loading and Saving Selections

What should you do if you've made a really complex selection and you'd like to save it? You should do just that. Save it!

With an area selected, you can save the selection in two ways. You can save the selection to disk, where it will remain until you need it later, or you can save the selection to an alpha channel. *Alpha channels* are special areas that keep selections. These channels are saved along with the file and can be reloaded later.

To save a selection as a file, choose Selections, Save to Disk. A standard Windows Save dialog box enables you to name and save the selection.

To save a selection as an alpha channel, choose Selections, Save as an Alpha Channel. This option opens the Save To Alpha dialog box in which you can choose the document to save the channel with and see the available channels (see Figure 5.12).

FIGURE 5.12.

The Save To Alpha dialog box.

After you select the document and click OK, you can name the selection. This option is handy if you'll be saving multiple selections with a document. After you save a selection, you can reload it into the current image. The nice thing about saving a selection to disk is that you can also load the selection into other images, as well.

To load a selection that you saved as a file, choose Selections, Load from Disk. This step brings up a standard Windows Open dialog box, where you can browse for and open any selection you previously saved.

To load a selection that has been saved as an alpha channel, choose Selections, Load from Alpha Channel. Doing so brings up the Load From Alpha dialog box, which enables you to choose the document and the channel you want to load (see Figure 5.13).

FIGURE 5.13.

The Load From Alpha dialog box.

Note that the Load From Alpha dialog box shows you a thumbnail preview of the selection, which comes in handy if you have saved several selections. Being able to visually choose the selection is a big plus if, like me, you're too lazy to name your selections as you save them.

Summary

Now that you've learned the basics of creating and editing selections, it's time to move on to Hour 6, "Working with Deformations."

Don't worry if you think that you haven't had much practice with selections. You'll be using selections constantly throughout the remainder of the book, and you'll soon have made enough of them to be considered an expert.

Workshop

The workshop contains a question and answer section to help answer the most commonly asked questions and quiz questions to help you solidify your understanding of the material covered.

Q&A

Q I have black text on a white background. I want to make the background blue. When I use Selections, Modify, Select Similar and then apply the Paint Bucket color to the white background, the insides of the letters don't turn blue! Why not?

A Even though the areas have been selected, the Paint Bucket tool may not fill in noncontiguous areas. To fill these extra areas, simply apply the Paint Bucket tool to them, as well.

5

Q I sometimes find the marquee distracting. Can I hide it and still keep the selection active?

A Yes, you can toggle the marquee on and off by choosing Selections, Hide Marquee or by pressing Shift+Ctrl+M. Hiding the marquee does not affect the selection.

Q Can I save a selection with the image instead of as a separate image?

A Yes. You can save a selection in an alpha channel. The alpha channel is saved along with the file if you save the image as a PSP, TIF, or PSD file.

Quiz

1. Name one way to make a selection from an image.
2. What does the Magic Wand tool do for you?
3. How can you add to a selection?
4. How can you subtract from a selection?

Answers

1. You can use the Selection tool to make a selection.
2. The Magic Wand tool enables you to make a selection based on the colors in an image.
3. You can add to a selection by holding down the Shift key while making subsequent selections.
4. You can subtract from a selection by holding down the Ctrl key while making subsequent selections.

HOUR 6

Working with Deformations

This hour introduces the following issues regarding working with deformations:

- Using the Deformation tool
- Resizing and rotating your images
- Adding perspective to images
- Using fadings and fills

You can use menu choices to resize, rotate, add perspective, and skew your images. Even better, though, you can apply these deformations to your images interactively. In this hour you learn how to apply these effects simply by clicking-and-dragging the mouse.

Using the Deformation Tool

If you can believe it, all of these cool deformations can be applied with one single tool! To see this tool in action, open a new 500×500, 72dpi image with a white background. Then follow these steps:

1. Set the foreground color to any color but white. I'm using black so that you can see the results easily as I work with the tool.

2. In the Layers palette, click the Add New Layer option to add a new layer over the background layer. I know we haven't covered layers yet, but you don't need to know how they work at this point.

3. In the Layer Properties dialog box, click OK.

4. Select the Text tool and click on the image.

5. In the Text tool dialog box, enter some text. The text you enter doesn't really matter; it could be your name, for example. Make sure that the size is large and that the Antialias and Floating checkboxes are checked. You can use any font and style you like (see Figure 6.1).

FIGURE 6.1.

The Add Text dialog box.

6. Click OK to place the text on the new layer (see Figure 6.2).

7. Select the Mover tool and use it to grab the text and move it to the center of the image.

8. Select the Deformation tool. When you select the Deformation tool, you'll notice a change in your image. A bounding box is added, and this bounding box has several control handles (see Figure 6.3).

9. As you move the mouse over the bounding box and the different control handles, the mouse pointer changes, too.

   If you move the mouse inside the bounding box away from any of the control handles, the pointer changes to a cross with an arrowhead at each end. This pointer enables you to move the selection along with the bounding box. Try it. Move the text around the image.

FIGURE 6.2.

Text on a new layer.

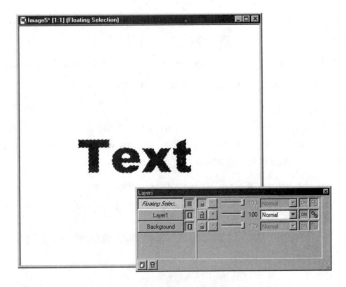

FIGURE 6.3.

Deformation tool's bounding box and control handles with the Layers palette shown.

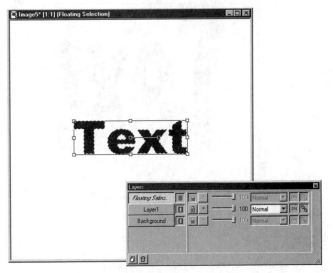

6

As you move the pointer, the bounding box follows; when you release the mouse button, the text snaps back inside the bounding box.

10. Move the pointer over one of the corner or the side handles.

As you move over a side handle, the mouse pointer becomes a two-headed arrow with a small rectangle above it. As you move the pointer over a corner handle, the mouse becomes a four-headed arrow (different from the four-headed arrow described previously) with a small rectangle over it.

Each type of control handle enables you to resize the bounding box, and the selection contained within it, interactively.

- With the side handles, you can adjust the width and height separately.
- With the corner handles, you can adjust the width and height of the selection simultaneously.

Try it. Move the mouse pointer over the one of the handles and click-and-drag it. As you do, you'll see the bounding box change shape. When you release the mouse button, the text resizes so that it fits into the box again.

If the resizing moves the text from the center of the image, just grab the text (or the bounding box, actually) and move it back into position (see Figure 6.4).

FIGURE 6.4.

Text enlarged with the Deformation tool.

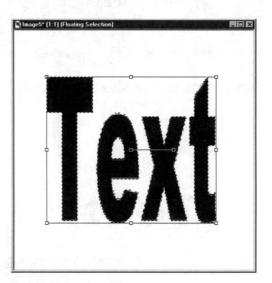

Rotating Text

With the text resized, try rotating it. Simply grab the right side of the center control handles and give it a spin. When you move the pointer over the control handle box, the mouse becomes a crosshair in the box and two circular arrows appear.

When you get it into position, double-click the mouse and, when the dialog box pops up, choose Yes to apply the deformation. You should have something similar to Figure 6.5.

FIGURE 6.5.

*Text rotated with the
Deformation tool.*

Using the Perspective, Shear, and Distort Options

In this section I use a practical application of the Deformation tool to demonstrate the Perspective, Shear, and Distort options. Follow these steps:

1. Open a new 500×500, 72dpi image with the background set to white.
2. Create a new layer by clicking the New Layer icon at the bottom of the Layers palette.
3. Set the foreground color to a mid to dark gray.
4. Select the Text tool and add some text as you did in the preceding example.
5. Choose Image, Flip to flip over the text (see Figure 6.6).
6. Select the Deformation tool and move the text to the right a little.
7. Grab the middle control handle along the bottom of the bounding box and drag down to resize the text vertically (see Figure 6.7).
8. Hold down the Ctrl key and drag the bottom-left corner down and out so that the bottom of the text gets larger while the top remains the same (see Figure 6.8). This is how you can add perspective to an image.

If the text seems to be running off the right side of the image, just drag the text toward the center with the mouse.

You can add a little shear to the text by holding down the Shift key while you drag any of the corners. I've sheared both bottom corners to the right a little (see Figure 6.9).

6

FIGURE 6.6.

*Text flipped over with
Image, Flip.*

FIGURE 6.7.

*Text resized with the
Deformation tool.*

With the deformations complete, choose Selections, Select None to deselect the text.
Then follow these steps:

1. Set the foreground color to something different than white or the color you used
   for the flipped, deformed text.

2. Select the Text tool and enter the same text with the same size and font settings
   that you used for the deformed text.

3. Position the text directly over the deformed text, as shown in Figure 6.10.

FIGURE 6.8.

Perspective added with the Deformation tool.

FIGURE 6.9.

Shear added with the Deformation tool.

6

Amazing! You've just created a much sought-after effect. You've created text with a perspective shadow.

FIGURE 6.10.

Text with a perspective shadow.

Adding a Shadow Effect

If you're daring enough, you can finish up this hour by making the shadow seem a little more realistic. To do so, you'll have to employ a technique from Hour 4, "Creating Your First Image," and use a new technique, as well. Follow these steps:

1. Access the Undo History command and back up to the point just before you added the new text. You should be at the point where you've just finished deforming the text.

2. Select the Dropper tool and click somewhere on the grey color of the text to set the foreground color to the grey you used for the shadow.

3. If the current background color, as seen in the foreground/background color swatches, is not white, use the Dropper tool to set it to white. To do so, right-click somewhere on the background of the image.

4. Select the Flood Fill tool.

5. In the Controls palette, click the Tool Controls tab.

6. Set the Fill Style to Linear Gradient, set the Match Mode to None, and click the Options button.

7. In the Flood Fill Options dialog box, set the direction to 180 degrees (see Figure 6.11).

8. Click anywhere in the selected text to fill it with the gradient. The letters should get paler as they get closer to the bottom of the image.

FIGURE 6.11.

Flood Fill Options dialog box.

9. Choose a foreground color and, using the Text tool, add the same text as you did before.

10. Maneuver the text into place over the perspective shadow (see Figure 6.12).

FIGURE 6.12.

Text with fading perspective shadow.

Wow! Now that is amazing! I consider this to be a fairly advanced technique, and here you've done it after only a few hours with the program.

Some other deformations are available under the Image, Deformations submenu. I cover these later, though, in relationship to filters.

6

Summary

Although this hour may have seemed long, it wasn't really. It's just that you covered quite a bit even if it was only with one tool. You've just created a really cool image and some text. Not bad for an hour's work.

I'd say that you're ready to head on to the next hour, where you learn how to use the drawing tools.

Workshop

The workshop contains a question and answer section to help answer the most commonly asked questions and quiz questions to help you solidify your understanding of the material covered.

Q&A

Q How do I know when I can apply a certain deformation, such as rotating the object?

A The mouse pointer changes as you move it over the various control handles. These changes signify when a deformation can be applied.

Q I enlarged an object using the Deformation tool and part of it is off the image window. How do I get it back?

A If the Deformation tool is still active, you can simply click-and-drag the object back into the center of the image. If you've applied the deformation, you can reactivate the Deformation tool and drag the object back into view.

Q How do I apply a deformation once I'm done?

A You can either click the Apply button in the Controls palette or double-click on the image and answer Yes in the dialog box that pops up.

Quiz

1. Explain how you enlarge a selection using the Deformation tool.

2. What is a bounding box? What can it help you do in relation to the Deformation tool?

3. How do you rotate an image with the Deformation tool?

4. How do you add perspective with the Deformation tool?

Answers

1. You can enlarge an object with the Deformation tool by dragging the middle control handles. The middle control handles are located at the center of the top, sides, and bottom of the bounding box.

2. The bounding box appears around an object when you activate the Deformation tool. It outlines the object that the deformations will affect.

3. You click-and-drag the handle near the middle of the bounding box. As you grab this control handle, the mouse pointer changes to a pair of semicircular curves with arrows at the ends.

4. You can add perspective by Ctrl+clicking-and-dragging one of the corner control handles.

6

Hour 7

Drawing Tools and Techniques

Paint Shop Pro provides a number of drawing tools. For example, you can use the Line tool to draw lines of various thicknesses, and you can use the various shapes tools to draw different shapes, such as rectangles and circles.

This hour introduces the following issues regarding drawing tools and techniques:

- Using the drawing tools options
- Drawing shapes
- Drawing normal lines
- Drawing Bézier lines

The Drawing Tools and Their Options

Like any other tools, the Line and Shapes tools have options that you can set to change the behavior of the tools. The Line tool has two styles. You can draw normal lines that are straight and go from one point on your image to another, and you can draw Bézier curves.

The Shapes tool is at the very bottom of the Tool palette, and the Line tool is directly above the Shapes tool. The Shapes tool icon has a small rectangle on it, and the Line tool icon has a small diagonal line across it.

Bézier curves are named for the French engineer, Bézier, who developed the mathematical theory for drawing these smooth curves in the 1970s.

As well as having two styles of drawing tools to choose from, you also can set the width of the lines and choose to have aliased or anti-aliased.

The shapes tools have a couple more options than the Line tool. You can choose from four shapes: rectangles, squares, ellipses, and circles. You can have the shape filled in the current foreground color or simply outlined. You can choose the thickness of the outline, and you can choose to have the shapes aliased or anti-aliased. The best way to see how these various options work is to roll up your sleeves and do a little drawing, so let's get started.

Drawing Shapes

To get a feeling for the Shapes tool, open a new 500×500 image with the resolution set to 72 pixels per inch, the background color set to white, and the image type set to 16.7 million colors. Then follow these steps:

1. Set the foreground color to anything but white and select the Shapes tool.

2. If the Controls palette is not visible, turn it on by clicking on the Controls Palette icon in the toolbar or by choosing View, Toolbars and placing a checkmark next to the Controls Palette option in the Toolbars dialog box.

   The Controls palette (see Figure 7.1) is where you can set the options that are available for the Shapes tool.

FIGURE 7.1.

The Controls palette.

3. Set the Shape to Circle, the Style to Filled, ignore the Outline Width for the moment, and place a checkmark in the Antialias checkbox.

4. Click-and-drag the mouse anywhere in your image, and you'll notice a circular outline being drawn.

5. Move the mouse until you get a good-sized circle and then release the mouse. When you release the mouse, a filled circle appears inside where the outline was (see Figure 7.2).

FIGURE 7.2.

Drawing a circle.

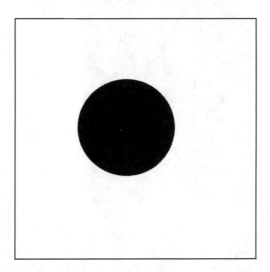

You'll notice that the circular shape is drawn from the center outward. Knowing this trick makes it easy to place your circles. How? Because you can place your cursor anywhere on the image by viewing the current mouse coordinates. In the bottom-left corner of the main Paint Shop Pro window is a set of numbers. These numbers are the current x and y coordinates of the mouse pointer.

To see how these coordinates work, move the mouse pointer onto the image and then look at the numbers as you move the mouse around the image window. The numbers constantly change as you move the mouse. You can use these numbers as a guide for placing the mouse pointer anywhere on your image.

To see how this technique works, follow these steps to draw a bull's-eye:

1. Choose Edit, Undo to undo the last circle that you drew.

2. Set the foreground color to black by moving the mouse pointer over the black area of the main color swatch and clicking. If you have trouble setting the color this

7

way, click the foreground color swatch to bring up the Color dialog box and set the color to black.

3. In the Color dialog box (see Figure 7.3), you can choose the color directly from the color grid if the color you want is there; you can also choose the color from the color wheel (and fine-tune it with the square inside the wheel), or you can enter the exact RGB values for the color. The RGB values for black are 0, 0, 0.

FIGURE 7.3.

The Color dialog box.

4. With the foreground color set to black, set the background color to red (you can do so by clicking on the background color swatch). The reason to set the two colors is that you can easily switch between them by clicking the small two-headed arrow to the lower left of the foreground/background color swatches. This technique makes it easy to use two colors without going back to the Color dialog box or guesstimating the colors with the main color swatch.

5. If you're not comfortable with moving the mouse into position by using the coordinates, you can turn on the grid. To do so, choose View, Grid. This action places a grid over the entire image (see Figure 7.4).

6. The default setting for the grid has a line every 10 pixels. You can change this setting to suit your needs for a particular image. To change the spacing of the grid, choose File, Preferences, General Program Preferences.

7. In the Paint Shop Pro Preferences dialog box, click the Rulers and Units tab to bring up the dialog box that enables you to set the Grid preferences (see Figure 7.5).

8. Change both the Horizontal and the Vertical Spacing to 50. This change gives you a more workable setting for drawing the bull's-eye.

FIGURE 7.4.

Image with grid visible.

FIGURE 7.5.

The Paint Shop Pro Preferences dialog box.

9. If you've chosen to go with the coordinates method, place the mouse pointer at the coordinates at 250,250 (the center of the image).

   If you're using the grid, move the mouse pointer to the center of the image where the gridlines cross.

10. Click-and-drag the mouse until you get a circle that's about 300 pixels in diameter. (You can see the diameter of the circle in the lower-left corner of the main window as you drag the mouse.)

    Along with the current coordinates, you get additional information in this portion of the main window. This information is very helpful when drawing or painting.

    The additional information depends on the particular tool you're using. For example, if you're using the Shapes tool to draw a rectangle, you will see the coordinates of the upper-left corner and the lower-left corner as well as the width and

7

height of the rectangle. If you're using the Line tool to draw a line, you'll see the starting and ending coordinates as well as the angle of the line.

11. Swap the foreground/background colors by clicking the small, two-headed arrow just below and to the left of the foreground/background color swatches.

12. Place the mouse back at the center of the image and draw another circle. Make this circle about 250 pixels in diameter. You should now have two concentric circles (see Figure 7.6).

FIGURE 7.6.

Partially completed bull's-eye.

13. Swap the foreground and background colors again and draw a third circle.

You can save a few mouse clicks when drawing your circles for the bull's-eye. To do so, simply draw the circles in the background color by clicking-and-dragging with the right mouse button. This great shortcut works in other situations as well. Click-and-drag with the left (primary) mouse button to draw with the foreground color; click-and-drag with the right (secondary) mouse button to draw with the background color.

14. Continue swapping the foreground and background colors and drawing smaller and smaller circles until the image contains five concentric circles (see Figure 7.7).

FIGURE 7.7.

Completed bull's-eye created with the Shapes tool.

15. Save this image so that you can load it later. To save the image, choose File, Save. Give the image a name (bullseye.psp will do nicely) and choose a folder to store it in. I often save files in a temporary folder if I think I'll need them to complete a drawing at a later sitting.

You might want to open a new file at this point and explore the other shapes that you can create with the Shapes tool. Try using different colors and drawing outlined shapes as well as filled shapes. Use the grid to help you place various shapes and try to draw something by combining the different shapes, colors, fills, and outlines.

Note how the rectangular and square shapes are drawn from a corner outward, unlike the circular and elliptical shapes, which are drawn from the center outward.

Drawing Lines

You can use the Line tool to draw straight lines and curved lines. You can set the width of the line and whether or not the line is anti-aliased in the Controls palette.

The Normal Line Tool

As an exercise, and to get some hands-on experience with the Line tool, you can add an arrow to the bull's-eye from the previous exercise.

Open the bull's-eye file that you saved and then follow these steps:

1. Set the foreground color to a shade of blue or some color other than the black and red that you used for the rings of the bull's-eye.

7

2. Select the Line tool and, in the Controls palette, set the Line Type to Normal, the Width to 12, and place a checkmark in the Antialias checkbox.

3. Place the mouse pointer near the center of the bull's-eye. Click-and-drag toward the upper-right corner of the image until the line goes past the outer circle of the bull's-eye (see Figure 7.8).

FIGURE 7.8.

Adding an arrow to the bull's eye with the Line tool.

4. Set the Line tool's Width to 2 and draw a smaller line perpendicular to the first line and across the first line about a third of the way up from the center of the bull's-eye (see Figure 7.9).

FIGURE 7.9.

Creating an arrowhead at the end of the line.

5. Draw two more lines that extend toward the center of the bull's-eye, starting at the ends of the cross line (see Figure 7.10).

FIGURE 7.10.

Completing the arrow-head lines.

6. You may want to zoom in to help with the placement of the lines. To do so, select the Zoom tool and click near the area that you're working on, in this case the center of the image. When you're zoomed in enough, reselect the Line tool and draw the lines.

7. To fill in the arrowhead, select the Flood Fill tool. In the Controls palette, set the Fill Style to Solid Color, the Match Mode to RGB, the Tolerance to about 10, and the Opacity to 100.

8. Click inside the areas of the arrowhead where the circles are showing through.

9. If the color leaks out to fill other parts of the drawing, choose Edit, Undo and set the Tolerance to a lower value.

10. The fill doesn't fill in the areas completely because of the anti-aliased lines that make up both the circles and the arrowhead.

    To fix this small problem, you can select the Paint Brushes tool and fill in the areas by hand. Select the Paint Brushes tool and, in the Controls palette, select the Brush Tip tab.

11. Set the Shape to Round, the Size to 1 or 2, the Opacity to 100, the Hardness to 0, and the Density to 100; ignore the Step setting for now.

12. Zoom in as much as you need to and fill in the areas that didn't get the color from the Flood Fill tool.

7

FIGURE 7.11.

Nearly completed arrowhead needing some touchups.

Your final image should resemble Figure 7.12.

FIGURE 7.12.

Final bull's-eye image, complete with arrow.

A while back, I created a banner to advertise a marketing group's web site. With the addition of a little text and a couple of special effects, you can use this image as a banner for your web site.

The Bézier Line Tool

The Bézier Line tool is a little harder to understand and control than the Normal Line tool. The Bézier tool is, however, a powerful addition to Paint Shop Pro and enables you to draw smooth curves that you couldn't draw with the older versions of this product.

Again, the best way to learn how to use this tool is to jump right in and draw some curves. Follow these steps:

1. Open a new 500×500 image with the resolution set to 72 pixels per inch, the background color set to white, and the image type set to 16.7 million colors.

2. Select the Line tool and, in the Controls palette, set the Style to Bézier and the Width to 10. Place a checkmark in the Antialias checkbox. You can turn the grid on or off for this exercise.

   In Figure 7.13, I've placed a couple of crosses with numbers to help you follow along as I show you how to draw your first Bézier curve.

FIGURE 7.13.

A couple of crosses to help with your first Bézier curve.

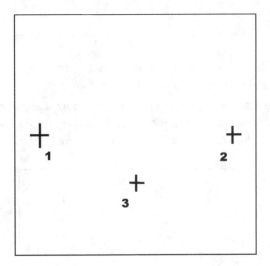

3. The Bézier curve Line tool requires a few mouse clicks (and a little magic) to draw your curve. Place your mouse pointer on your image at approximately the position of the first cross in Figure 7.13.

   Click-and-drag the mouse over to a point that's about where I've placed the second cross in Figure 7.13 and release the mouse button.

4. Move the mouse pointer to about where I've drawn the third cross and click-and-hold the mouse button. A smooth curve should appear (see Figure 7.14).

7

FIGURE 7.14.

Drawing a smooth Bézier curve with the Line tool.

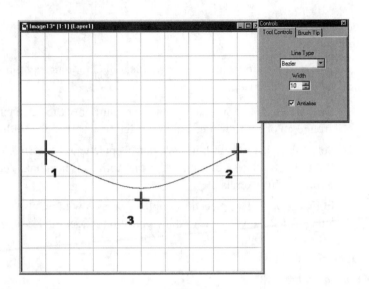

5. Now move the mouse around without releasing the button. You should see the curve bend and twist as you move the mouse around.

   After you release the mouse and click it once more, the curve will be drawn in the width that you've specified in the Controls palette (see Figure 7.15). Be sure to click near the third cross so that your curve resembles the one in Figure 7.15.

FIGURE 7.15.

A smooth Bézier curve drawn with the Line tool.

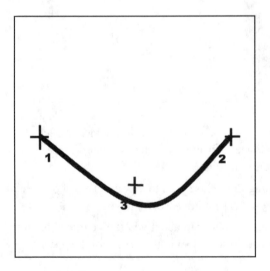

Points 1 and 2 are the endpoints of the curve, and point 3 is the control point. You can use this method to create semicircular curves.

To create S-curves, click once in the third position and then click again above and to the right or left of the middle of the first two points.

> You can draw lines in either the current foreground color or the current background color. To draw in the foreground color, click-and-drag with the primary mouse button. To draw in the current background color, click-and-drag with the right mouse button.

You should spend some time learning how this tool works. It is a powerful addition to Paint Shop Pro and learning how to use it will give you an edge over other Paint Shop Pro artists. Figure 7.16 shows some curves drawn with the Bézier Line tool.

FIGURE 7.16.

Some S-shape and semicircular curves drawn with the Bézier Line tool.

Summary

In this hour you learned how to draw shapes, lines, and curves. You've seen how to use the coordinates and the other information that is displayed at the lower-left corner of the main window, and you've learned how to use the grid feature and how to set its options.

You're about ready to move on to the next hour, where you'll learn how to use the painting tools.

7

Workshop

The workshop contains a question and answer section to help answer the most commonly asked questions and quiz questions to help you solidify your understanding of the material covered.

Q&A

Q Is it possible to draw triangles with the Shapes tool?

A No. You can make triangles and other polygons with the Line tool and fill them in with the Flood Fill tool, though.

Q Can I change the color of the lines that make up the grid?

A Yes. In the Paint Shop Pro Preferences dialog box (choose File, Preferences, General Program Preferences) under the Rulers and Units tab, you can set the line spacing and the color of the grid lines.

Q Is it possible to determine the angle of the line that I'm drawing with the Line tool?

A Yes. At the lower-left corner of the screen, this piece of information is available as you're using the drawing tools. Note that straight up is 0 degrees and that the angle increases as you go clockwise.

Q Can I use the Shapes tool to draw complex shapes other than rectangles, squares, ellipses, and circles?

A Yes, you can draw complex shapes by drawing several simpler shapes on top of each other. By combining shapes and colors, you can draw almost anything.

Quiz

1. Which basic shapes are available with the Shapes tool?
2. How do you draw a line or a shape in the current background color?
3. How many different shapes of curves can be drawn with the Bézier Line tool?
4. How do you draw a line with the Line tool?

Answers

1. The Shapes tool provides these basic shapes: rectangle, square, ellipse, and circle.
2. Click-and-drag the mouse while holding down the secondary mouse button.
3. Two. You can draw semicircular and S-shape curves with the Bézier Line tool.
4. Click-and-drag from where you want the line to begin to where you want the line to end.

HOUR 8

Painting Tools and Techniques

This hour introduces the following issues regarding Paint Shop Pro's painting tools:

- Painting and drawing with the Paint Brushes tool
- Using the Airbrush tool
- Using the Flood Fill tool
- Working with the Clone Brush tool

Paint Shop Pro provides a number of painting tools: the Paintbrush, the Airbrush, the Flood Fill, and the Clone Brush tools. In this hour you learn how to use these tools effectively.

Some readers may consider the Picture Tube a painting tool, and rightly so. However, the Picture Tube is complex enough to deserve its own hour. You learn all about the Picture Tube tool in Hour 14, "Picture Tubes."

Painting and Drawing with the Paint Brushes Tool

The Paint Brushes tool (the tenth tool from the top in the Tool palette; it looks like a small paintbrush) enables you to draw and paint freehand lines with a variety of brushes and textures. After selecting the Paint Brushes tool, you can set the various options in the Controls palette (see Figure 8.1).

FIGURE 8.1.

The Controls palette showing the controls for the Paint Brushes tool.

Using the Tool Controls

From within the Controls palette, under the Brush Tip tab, you can set the shape and the brush type. You can also set the size, opacity, hardness, density, and step. Clicking on the Brush Options icon (to the right of the Shape drop-down box) displays a pull-down menu from which you can select the brush type.

Under the Tool Controls tab, you can select a texture to be used with the brush.

To see how these settings work, open a new 500×500 image with the resolution set to 72 pixels per inch, the background color set to white, and the image type set to 16.7 million colors. Then follow these steps:

1. Select the Paint Brushes tool.

2. Set the foreground color to a pale blue.

3. In the Controls palette, set Shape to Round, the brush options to normal, Size to 13, Opacity to 100, Hardness to 50, Density to 100, and Step to 25. Some of these settings may not need to be set, because they are the defaults.

4. Click-and-drag in the image to draw a line (see Figure 8.2).

5. Increase the Size setting to 45 and decrease the Hardness setting to 20. If you have a little trouble getting these exact numbers by moving the slider, don't worry about it. Either get as close as you can or click in the small window to the right of the slider and enter the value.

FIGURE 8.2.

Drawing a line with the Paint Brushes tool.

6. Draw another line. Compared to the first line, the new line is larger and its edges are softer (see Figure 8.3).

FIGURE 8.3.

Drawing a larger, softer line with the Paint Brushes tool.

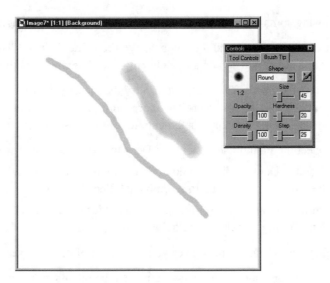

7. Set the foreground color to a bright yellow and change the brush option so that the brush is a pencil.

8. Set Opacity to about 30 and then draw another line that passes over the first two.

The mark made by the pencil is different from the mark made by the brush. In addition, you can see the first two lines through the third line (see Figure 8.4).

FIGURE 8.4.

Drawing a third line with the Paint Brushes tool set to a pencil and with a lower opacity.

Try drawing some lines with the other options. Each is a different brush shape.

Try varying the opacity and the color that you're using. If you'd like to draw with the background color, you can do so by clicking-and-dragging with the right mouse button.

When you've drawn a few lines, you can try the Density control. Density controls how much paint the brush lays down. The more dense, the more paint is laid down. To see how the Density setting controls the output, follow these steps:

1. Select the Paintbrush option; the Density setting should move to 100.

2. Drag the Density slider so that the density is set to about 50, and you'll notice that the brush preview starts to resemble the Pencil brush.

3. Draw a line with this setting and compare it to one of the lines you drew with the Pencil option. The lines are quite similar.

Changing the various settings gives you quite a bit of control over the Paint Brushes tool.

The Step setting is a bit more mysterious than the other settings. It works in combination with a brush's diameter. The "step" is a percentage of the diameter of the brush. For example, with the brush Size set to 30 and the Step set to 30, the brush operates at 100 percent and draws a definite line (because 30 is 100 percent of 30).

8

With the Size set to 30 and the Step set to 60, the brush paints only 50 percent of the time (because 30 is 50 percent of 60; see Figure 8.5).

FIGURE 8.5.

The left line shows the Step option at 100 percent (both brush Size and Step set to 30), and the right line shows the Step option at 50 percent (brush Size set to 30 and Step set to 60).

As you increase the step relative to the brush size, less paint is used.

Play around with the brush Size and the Step settings until you're comfortable.

Custom Brush Tips

You've seen how the various controls work, and you've used several brush tips. You can also use some custom brushes to create new effects.

Click the Brush Options icon and, from the pull-down menu, choose Custom. Use the Custom Brush dialog box to select a custom brush (see Figure 8.6).

FIGURE 8.6.

The Custom Brush dialog box.

Choose one of the brushes and click-and-drag within the image. The pattern you've chosen is used as a brush for the lines you're drawing.

Figure 8.7 shows some paint strokes drawn with the leaf brush in various colors.

FIGURE 8.7.

*The Custom Brush tool
used to draw some
leaves in different
colors.*

You may notice that some of the settings for the Paint Brushes tool are greyed-out in the Controls palette. These tools are not available for use with this particular brush.

Practice using some of the brushes. When you're done, you can set the Paint Brushes tool back to Normal or to one of the other options.

Using Different Textures

Along with the different tips and other settings, you can choose from several textures.

You can choose a texture from the Controls palette by clicking the Tool Controls tab and choosing from the pull-down menu. Choices include Sidewalk, Marble, Parchment, Fruit Peel, Construction Paper, Ocean, Lava, Mist, and Fog.

To see how the textures work, click the Tool Controls tab and choose a texture. When you draw or paint, the texture appears under your brushstrokes. In Figure 8.8, the Woodgrain texture has been applied with a very wide paintbrush.

FIGURE 8.8.

Woodgrain texture applied with a wide paintbrush.

8

Using the Airbrush Tool

The Airbrush tool allows paint to build up if you stay in one place for a moment. Note that the paint buildup isn't a selectable option; rather, it is the behavior of the Airbrush tool.

To see how the airbrush effect works, select the Airbrush tool (the fifth icon from the bottom in the Tool palette; it looks like a spray can) and draw a few lines, stopping every so often. When you stop, keep the mouse button down; you'll notice that the paint builds up. This effect is more noticeable with the opacity set fairly low. Even with the opacity set low, the brush will build up paint until it completely covers whatever is beneath it.

Other than that, the Airbrush tool acts much like the other Paint Brushes tools. You can still change the various options and settings in the Controls palette and you can still use the textures.

Using the Flood Fill Tool

You can use the Flood Fill tool (the fourth icon from the bottom of the Tool palette; it looks like a tilted paint can) to fill areas of an image with either a color, a gradient, or a pattern.

Filling an Area with a Solid Color

To fill an area with a solid color, you can simply set the foreground or background color to the color you want to use and click within the area you want to fill. Clicking with the left mouse button fills with the foreground color and clicking with the right mouse button fills with the background color.

Several factors determine how the Flood Fill tool fills in an area. If you've made a selection and you click within the selected area, the Flood Fill tool fills that area. If you've made a selection and you click outside the selection, even if you've chosen to hide the selection marquee, the Flood Fill tool has no effect.

You can also click in an area that already contains a certain color. The Flood Fill tool will then fill the area that contains that color. It may fill surrounding areas depending on the settings you've chosen. Changing the Tolerance option, for example, can determine how much of an area is filled. A higher tolerance allows more of an area to be filled, whereas a lower tolerance constrains the fill to areas that are similar in color or exactly the same color as where you initially click. You can change the Tolerance setting in the Controls palette under the Tool Controls tab.

The Match mode also affects how an area is filled. Selecting RGB compares neighboring pixels' RGB values, selecting Hue compares neighboring pixels' hues, selecting Brightness compares neighboring pixels' brightness values, and selecting none fills the entire area regardless of any settings. You can change the Match Mode setting in the Controls palette under the Tool Controls tab. Once a comparison has been made according to the Match mode, a pixel will be filled according to the Tolerance setting.

You can also choose the Flood Fill tool's opacity. A higher value makes the fill more opaque, and a lower value makes the fill more transparent. The Sample Merged option has to do with layers; I cover that option in Hour 11, "Layers."

Finally, you can set the options for each fill style by clicking the Options button. Each fill style has different options associated with it. For example, you can set the direction of a linear gradient fill.

Filling with a Gradient

In addition to filling an area with a solid color, you can fill it with a gradient. A *gradient* is a blend from one color to another. Paint Shop Pro blends from the current foreground to the current background color.

Figure 8.9 shows the styles of gradients that are available in Paint Shop Pro.

8

FIGURE 8.9.

Paint Shop Pro has several gradient fills.

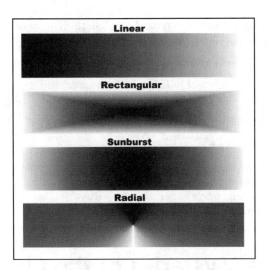

You can set the angle for the Linear Gradient, and you can set the Horizontal and Vertical starting points for the Rectangular, Sunburst, and Radial gradients. To access these options, click the Options button under the Tool Controls tab in the Controls palette.

I demonstrate some of the uses for gradients in later chapters. For now, you can experiment with this setting to see the effect it has on the gradient.

Filling with a Pattern

You can also use the Flood Fill tool to fill an area with a pattern. To set the pattern, select the Flood Fill tool and click the Tools Control tab in the Controls palette.

Set the Fill Style to Pattern and click the Options button to bring up the Flood Fill Options dialog box (see Figure 8.10).

FIGURE 8.10.

The Flood Fill Options dialog box.

You can select any open image from the New Pattern Source pull-down menu. If some part of the current image is selected when you choose the pull-down menu, the selected area will be chosen as the pattern.

This option enables you to quickly fill an area or an entire image with a predefined pattern. If the area you're filling is larger than the pattern you've selected, the pattern will tile over the selected area.

Because the pattern fill repeats in the same manner as a web page background, you can get a good idea of how your tiles will look. Simply create a new image that's larger than the pattern and use the Flood Fill tool to fill the image with the pattern.

Learning the Mysteries of the Clone Brush Tool

The Clone Brush (the tenth tool from the bottom of the Tool palette; it resembles two paintbrushes) is a mysterious and powerful tool. You can use the Clone Brush tool to paint over a portion of an image with another area of the same image, an area from another open image, and one layer to another.

In Figure 8.11 I've started cloning the image in the foreground into the image in the background. The image in the background was opened as a new file with a white background. I then opened the file I wanted to clone and set the texture of the Clone Brush tool to Woodgrain.

I activated the Clone Brush tool by right-clicking in the image at the position where I wanted to clone from.

All I needed to do to draw a clone of the bird was to draw in the new image by clicking-and-dragging. Because of the texture feature, I got a nice artsy-looking clone of the bird in the new image.

The Clone Brush can also remove blemishes from portraits, remove telephone wires from photographs, and retouch images. I demonstrate this tool in more depth in Hour 17, "Retouching Your Images."

The options available for the Clone Brush tool, under the Tool Controls tab in the Controls palette, are Aligned and Non-Aligned. You can also set a texture for the brush.

FIGURE 8.11.

Using the Clone Brush tool to "paint" one image into another.

8

The Aligned option moves the source area relative to the original area you choose even if you release the mouse and then start to clone again. The Non-Aligned option restarts the source area from the original area you choose if you release the mouse and start again.

Summary

In this hour you learned how to use Paint Shop Pro's many painting tools. I've just hinted at the real power of some of these tools. As you work through the rest of this book, you'll learn to apply this power.

In the next hour you learn how to use color effectively in the images you create with Paint Shop Pro.

Workshop

The workshop contains a question and answer section to help answer the most commonly asked questions and quiz questions to help you solidify your understanding of the material covered.

Q&A

Q Can I use different textures within the same image?

A Yes, you can use as many textures as you want. All you need to do is change the texture setting in the Tool Controls palette before you add a new effect.

Q How do I change the size of a Paint Brushes tool?

A You can change the size of a Paint Brushes tool, along with its other options, in the Controls palette.

Q When I make a selection for use with the Pattern option of the Flood Fill tool, do I need to use Edit, Copy to set the pattern?

A No. All you need to do is select the image with the active selection from the pull-down menu in the Flood Fill Options dialog box.

Q How do I paint with the current background color?

A You can paint with the current background color by clicking-and-dragging with the secondary mouse button (normally the right mouse button).

Quiz

1. What are the differences between the Airbrush tool and the Paint Brushes tool?
2. Can you use the Clone Brush tool to clone from one image to another? How?
3. What does the Density setting in the Paint Brushes tool do?
4. What does the Opacity setting in the Paint Brushes tool do?
5. What effect does the Tolerance setting have on how an area is filled with the Flood Fill tool?

Answers

1. The Airbrush tool lays down more paint if held in one spot for any length of time.
2. Yes. Open both images. Then right-click on the image you want to clone from and paint in the image you want to clone to.
3. The Density setting in the Paint Brushes tool determines how much paint is laid down with each stroke. Increasing and decreasing the density effectively adds and removes bristles from the brush.
4. The Opacity setting in the Paint Brushes tool determines how much of the underlying image is visible through the application of the painting tool. A setting of 1 is almost transparent, whereas a setting of 100 is totally opaque.
5. The Tolerance setting determines whether a pixel will be filled based on its value compared to its neighbor. This setting goes hand in hand with the Match Mode setting.

HOUR 9

Using Color Effectively

This hour introduces the following issues regarding the use of color:

- Using the color tools
- Learning the color models used with Paint Shop Pro
- Adjusting shadows, highlights, and midtones
- Adjusting hue, saturation, and luminance

As you would expect, color is extremely important to digital art. Paint Shop Pro provides several ways of choosing and adjusting colors. In this hour you learn how to choose and adjust colors effectively.

The Color Tools

Paint Shop Pro offers several ways to choose and adjust the colors you use to create and edit your images. You can choose from the colors that exist in an image, and you can choose new colors in a number of ways.

To choose colors from an existing image, you use the Dropper tool. To set new foreground and background colors, you use the Color palette.

Using the Dropper Tool

The Dropper tool (shaped like an eyedropper) is one of the easiest tools to use. To use the Dropper tool, simply select it and move it over an existing image. As you move the Dropper tool over the image, the color that the tool is over appears in the bottom of the Color palette.

Clicking the left (or primary) mouse button sets the current foreground color to the color under the Dropper tool; clicking the right (or secondary) mouse button sets the current background color to the color under the Dropper tool.

Using the Dropper tool is a great way to pick certain colors from an image for use in the same, or another, image.

Using the Color Palette

The Color palette (see Figure 9.1) is where you pick new foreground and background colors from scratch.

FIGURE 9.1.

The Color palette.

The Color palette has three parts:

- First is the main color swatch. You can use this area of the Color palette to quickly choose a new foreground or background color. To choose a new color from the main color swatch, simply move the mouse pointer around the main swatch until the color you want appears in the new color swatch at the bottom of the Color palette.

  To set the color you see displayed in the new color swatch to the current foreground color, left-click the mouse. To set the color you see displayed in the new color swatch to the current background color, right-click the mouse. It's as simple as that. Unfortunately, getting exactly the right color in this manner is a little tricky. I'll show you a more exact method in a moment.

- The second part of the Color palette contains the current foreground/background color swatches. There is also a small, two-headed arrow to the lower left of the twin swatches. Clicking the two-headed arrow swaps the current foreground and background colors. The arrows act as a toggle, meaning that each time you click the icon, the foreground and background colors will change places.

The twin swatches do more than just show you the current foreground and background colors, though. Clicking either one brings up the Color dialog box. I'll get back to this in a moment.

- Below the foreground/background color swatches is a small RGB readout. This readout displays the RGB values (for red, green, and blue, the most common way of describing the colors used with computer displays) for the color that the mouse pointer is over in the main color swatch. This color is displayed in the new color swatch.

The Paint Shop Pro Color Dialog Box

To bring up the Color dialog box and subsequently use it to choose a new color, simply click on either the foreground or the background color swatch.

Either the Paint Shop Pro Color dialog box or the standard Windows Color dialog box appears, depending on your selection in the Paint Shop Pro Preferences dialog box. If you haven't specified a Color dialog box, Paint Shop Pro defaults to its own (see Figure 9.2).

FIGURE 9.2.

The Paint Shop Pro Color dialog box.

 If you've chosen to work on an image with 256 or fewer colors or an image that is greyscale, you'll get a Color palette instead of a Color dialog box. Color palettes are limited to 256 colors or shades of grey.

The Paint Shop Pro dialog box is, in my opinion, the better choice here. It's much easier to zero in on a color using this Color dialog box than it is with the Windows Color dialog box. The Paint Shop Pro Color dialog box contains several areas:

- In the upper right is the color wheel. You can choose an approximate color from the color wheel.

- Inside the color wheel is the Saturation/Lightness box. You use this area to fine-tune your color selection.

- At the upper left is a set of basic colors that you can choose from. Below the basic colors is an area where you can store your own custom colors by clicking on the Add Custom button.

- At the lower right is a swatch that displays the current color.

- At the lower left is a series of numbers. You'll find the RGB and the HSL (Hue, Saturation, and Lightness), as well as the HTML number (or hexadecimal value) of the color you're choosing from the color wheel and the Saturation/Lightness box.

In addition to seeing the values for any color in the RGB, HSL, and HTML number areas, you can set the values for a particular color manually. This is true for the RGB area on the Color palette, as well.

The Windows Color Dialog Box

If you prefer to use the Windows Color dialog box, you can do so. To set the preferences to bring up the Windows Color dialog box, choose File, Preferences, General Program Preferences. In the Paint Shop Pro Preferences dialog box, click the Dialogs and Palettes tab (see Figure 9.3).

FIGURE 9.3.

The Paint Shop Pro Preferences dialog box showing the Dialogs and Palettes tab.

If you place a checkmark in the Use Standard Windows Color Picker checkbox, the next time you click on either the foreground or background color swatch, you'll get the Windows Color dialog box (see Figure 9.4) instead of the Paint Shop Pro Color dialog box.

FIGURE 9.4.

The Windows Color dialog box.

9

The main difference between the Windows Color dialog box and the Paint Shop Pro Color dialog box is how you go about choosing new colors.

With the Windows Color dialog box, you choose an approximate color from the main color swatch and then fine-tune it with the slider to the right of the color swatch. I find this method less exacting than using the Paint Shop Pro Color dialog box. Because the result is the same, though, the choice is up to you.

The Color Models Used with Paint Shop Pro

Because Paint Shop Pro is geared more toward onscreen imaging than toward high-end printing, the main color mode is RGB. Paint Shop Pro does use two other methods, as well. You can use CMYK, which is used in the printing industry, and HSL, which is another way of describing RGB colors. Each of these methods is discussed in the following sections.

The RGB Model

RGB (for Red, Green, and Blue) is a method of describing the colors that you see on your computer screen. Each of the three colors can have a value ranging from 0 to 255, for a total of 256 values.

If you multiply the three total values together (256×256×256) you get 16,777,216 or 16.7 million colors. Look familiar? It should. It is one of the image types you can choose when you open a new file. The 16.7 million colors that you can see on your screen are made up of combinations of red, green, and blue.

For example, the value 255, 0, 0 is bright red. This color is made up of 255 parts red, no green, and no blue. The color 0, 255, 0 is bright green because there is no red, 255 parts green, and no blue. What color do you think you'd get from 0, 0, 255? If you said bright blue, you are right.

If you combine 255 parts red with 255 parts green and no blue, you get a bright yellow. If you mix no red, 255 parts green, and 255 parts blue, you get a bright pale blue or cyan.

Mixing 255 parts red with no green and 255 parts blue yields a bright purple or magenta.

Setting all the values to 255 gives you white, whereas setting them all to 0 gives you black. This brings up the interesting question: How do you get the shades of grey?

Easy! Any time all of the values are equal, you'll get a shade of grey. From 0, 0, 0 (black) to 255, 255, 255 (white) you have the possibility of 254 shades of grey. The greys range from a very dark (almost black) grey (1, 1, 1) to a very light (almost white) grey (254, 254, 254) and all the shades of grey you'll need.

A nice medium grey can be entered as 128, 128, 128—right in middle between 0, 0, 0, and 255, 255, 255. You might want to open up the Color dialog box and enter some values for R, G, and B to see how the colors are affected.

The CMYK Model

The CMYK (for Cyan, Magenta, Yellow, and a percentage of blacK) model is used with printing inks. Cyan, magenta, and yellow inks are mixed to produce the various colors used to reproduce images on printers.

When cyan, magenta, and yellow inks are mixed, they produce black. However, it's very difficult to produce true black because of impurities in these inks. This is where the black ink comes in. By adding various amounts of black ink, you can get richer tones and deeper, darker blacks.

Normally, before printing an image in CMYK, you separate the image into different plates. Each plate contains one of the CMYK colors. When combined, the four plates reproduce your color images on high-end color printers.

Unless you'll be doing high-end printing of your digital images, you'll probably never have to use the CMYK model.

The HSL Model

The HSL (for Hue, Saturation, and Lightness) model is another way of looking at RGB colors. The HSL model, which is a more natural way of describing colors (at least in terms of humans versus computers), is fairly easy to understand.

To set a color with this mode, you choose a color or *Hue*, from 0 to 255. You then set the *Saturation*, or amount of color and finally, you set the *Lightness*, or brightness of the color.

Hues start at 0 (red) and move through brown, yellow, green, light blue, dark blue, purple, and finally back to red.

If you look at the color wheel in the Paint Shop Pro Color dialog box, you'll notice that the top of the wheel is red, and it then moves counterclockwise through the progression.

Saturation sets how much color you see. A lower setting makes the color more grey, and a higher setting yields a brighter color.

The Lightness value determines how bright or dark a color is. A lower number means less light and, therefore, a darker color, whereas a higher number means more light and a brighter color.

You can try changing the HSL values in the Color dialog box to see how the values affect the different colors.

Adjusting Shadows, Highlights, and Midtones

You can use the Highlight, Midtone, and Shadow controls to adjust the overall tonal range of an image or to correct an image's tones separately. You access this command from the Colors, Adjust, Highlight/Midtone/Shadow menu.

To see how the tones of an image are distributed, you can view the image's histogram. Click the Histogram Palette icon on the toolbar to bring up the Histogram palette (see Figure 9.5). (The Histogram Palette icon is the third-to-last icon on the standard toolbar at the top of the Paint Shop Pro window.)

FIGURE 9.5.

The Histogram palette showing an image's luminance.

The Histogram palette shows the distribution of pixels throughout an image. You can see the distribution of the red, green, and blue pixels as well as the distribution of the luminance. In Figure 9.5, I've chosen to view only the Luminance values.

You can see that the image that this histogram represents is a high-key image. A *high-key image* is a bright or fairly light image.

The image that this histogram is reporting on also appears in Figure 9.5. The bird is mostly white, and a lot of highlights are on the water. You can use the histogram to help you decide how to adjust an image.

Armed with the histogram's graph, you can decide whether you need to adjust the highlights, the shadows, or the midtones, or a combination of the three.

As stated earlier, you choose Colors, Adjust, Highlight/Midtone/Shadow to make the tonal adjustments. In the Highlight/Midtone/Shadow dialog box (see Figure 9.6), you can adjust each tonal range separately.

FIGURE 9.6.

The Highlight/Midtone/ Shadow dialog box.

Because you can adjust the different ranges separately, you can use this dialog box to emphasize the highlights or shadows and to darken or lighten the midtones.

You're provided with a real-time preview so that you can see the results of the changes you make. You can also turn on the Auto Proof option, which enables you to see the changes in the actual image.

Having the Auto Proof option on can affect the speed at which your changes take place. If this option slows you down, you can leave the Auto Proof option off and simply click the Proof button when you want to see the effect of your changes on the image.

If you've ever scanned images into your computer only to find that they are too light or too dark, you can use the Highlight/Midtone/Shadow dialog box to adjust the images.

Adjusting Hue, Saturation, and Luminance

Just as you can affect the tones of an image with the Highlight/Midtone/Shadow dialog box, you can adjust the hue, saturation, and luminance of an image with the Hue/Saturation/Lightness dialog box (see Figure 9.7). You access this dialog box by choosing Colors, Adjust, Hue/Saturation/Luminance.

FIGURE 9.7.

The Hue/Saturation/Lightness dialog box.

If an image has a color cast, is too bright overall, or is dull or overly saturated, you can use the controls in the Hue/Saturation/Lightness dialog box to make adjustments to the image.

Again, you're provided with a real-time preview so that you can see the results of the changes before applying them to the image.

You can use the Hue/Saturation/Lightness adjustments to create a sepia-toned image. If you have a color image you'd like to try this technique on, open it in Paint Shop Pro. Then follow these steps:

1. Choose Colors, Adjust, Hue/Saturation/Luminance.
2. Set the Hue to around 50 and the Saturation to about –70.
3. Click on the Proof button, and you should see your image take on a sepia tone.

What has happened is that you removed a lot of the saturation so that the image is more like a black-and-white photo. There is still enough color to show the hue, though, which you've changed to a brownish shade. This effect was, and still is, a popular photo effect. Give it a try!

Summary

In this hour you learned how to choose colors from an existing image and how to effectively use the Color dialog boxes to set new colors. In addition, you learned a little about correcting and enhancing an image's highlights, midtones, and shadows. You also saw how to adjust the hue, saturation, and luminance of an image. Try experimenting with these setting until you are comfortable using them.

Note that Hour 21, "Preparing Your Graphics for the Web," covers the color issues that you'll need to understand to reproduce your images effectively on the web. In the next hour, you'll learn how to create some really cool text effects with Paint Shop Pro.

Workshop

The workshop contains a question and answer section to help answer the most commonly asked questions and quiz questions to help you solidify your understanding of the material covered.

Q&A

Q When I'm following along with the examples in the book, how can I enter the exact colors you're using?

A You can enter the exact RGB values I use in the RGB area of the Color dialog box.

Q Why would I want to toggle the foreground/background colors?

A Toggling the colors makes it easier to use two colors. With the foreground/background color swatches available in the Color palette, you can swap colors with one mouse click.

Q You said that you preferred the Paint Shop Pro Color dialog box to the Windows Color dialog box. Why?

A I just find it easier to get exactly the color I want with the Paint Shop Pro color wheel and Saturation/Lightness box. You can try both and see which one works best for you. The result will be the same—choosing the right color for the job.

Q How do I interpret the graph in the Histogram palette?

A The histogram depicts the colors and luminance of an image, and the graph varies for each image. The graph represents the distribution of pixels in an image. The lighter pixels are represented at the right, and the darker ones at the left. If an image is too light, the graph rises at the right. If an image is too dark, the graph rises to the left. You can decide, based on the graph, how to adjust an image. Then you can use the Highlight/Midtone/Shadow controls to adjust your image.

Quiz

1. What's one way to quickly choose a new foreground color?

2. How can you quickly set an exact foreground or background color?

3. What is the difference between the Paint Shop Pro Color dialog box and the Windows Color dialog box?

4. How can you enhance the shadows of an image without affecting the midtones and highlights?

Answers

1. By clicking (left to set the foreground and right to set the background) in the main color swatch in the Color palette.

2. By clicking in either the foreground or background color swatch and setting the values manually in the RGB section of the Color dialog box.

3. The main difference is how you select a color. You use a swatch and a slider in the Windows Color dialog box; you use a color wheel and a Saturation/Lightness box in the Paint Shop Pro Color dialog box.

4. By adjusting the Shadow slider in the Highlight/Midtone/Shadow dialog box.

9

Hour 10

Creating Cool Text Effects

This hour introduces the following issues regarding cool text effects:

- Using the Text tool
- Creating wooden-textured text
- Creating chrome text
- Adding a drop shadow
- Adding glow to your text

Paint Shop Pro enables you to enter text into your images via the Text tool. No explicit special effects are built into the Text tool. However, with a little ingenuity and the application of some of the other Paint Shop Pro tools and effects, you can create some amazing effects with text.

Using the Text Tool

The Text tool, itself, is straightforward and easy to use. To add text to your images, simply select the Text tool (the button with the big A on it) and click where you want the text to be in your image. Doing so brings up the Add Text dialog box (see Figure 10.1).

FIGURE 10.1.

The Add Text dialog box.

In the Add Text dialog box, you can select the name, style, size, and script of a font. You can choose whether or not to underline, strike out, or anti-alias your text.

 If the color resolution of your image is 256 colors or less, the Antialias option is greyed-out and you won't be able to select it. You should generally create your images and work on them with higher color resolutions, preferably 16.7 million colors.

You can choose the alignment of your text and decide whether it should float. Last, but not least, you can enter the text itself.

The Add Text dialog box shows you a preview of the text as you enter it. You can see the font and style, and you can get an idea of the size of the text, as well.

 You may notice that the predefined sizes in the Add Text dialog box are limited. However, you can simply enter whatever value you want in the window above the Size box. This method helps if, for example, you want to use a font size that's bigger than the largest predefined size of 72 points.

After you've chosen your font, its size, style, and script; decided whether it should be anti-aliased; and entered the actual text, what then? Why, you get to play around with it and see what kind of weird and wonderful things you can do to it.

Creating Wooden-Textured Text

You can use some of the built-in textures along with a filter or two and some selection manipulation to create some pretty cool text effects. This next exercise shows you how to create a textured wood effect. Follow these steps:

1. Open a new 500×200-pixel image with the resolution set to 72 pixels per inch. Set the background color to white and the image type to 16.7 million colors.

2. Set the foreground color to white and the background color to a medium brown. I chose R: 165, G: 92, B:5. If you need to refresh your memory on how to set the foreground and background colors, refer to Hour 9, "Using Color Effectively."

   You may notice that I'm about to add white text to a white background, and you may be wondering why I chose this combination. The reason is that I intend to paint over the text with a new color and a texture. Having the white text on the white background allows some of the white background to show through the texture, which is exactly what I want to have happen.

3. Select the Text tool and, in the Add Text dialog box, set the options as follows:

   Name: Arial Black

   Style: Regular

   Script: Western

   Size: 72

   Text Effects: Antialias (This setting makes the text nice and smooth.)

   Alignment: Left (Although this setting really matters only when you're entering more than one line of text.)

4. Then place a checkmark in the Floating checkbox.

   I always select the Floating option so that I can easily move the text into position. However, this feature won't matter as much when the text is on its own layer.

   If you don't use the Floating option, the text comes in looking the same. However, if you move the text, you leave behind a hole in the image that gets filled with the background color. This is true only when there is something already on the layer that you're adding the text to.

5. All that said, let's get back to creating some wooden text. Type in the text that you want to use. With a little thought, I came up with the word *Wooden*.

10

In Figure 10.2, you can see that the text comes into the image surrounded by the selection marquee.

FIGURE **10.2.**

White-on-white text
surrounded by the
selection marquee.

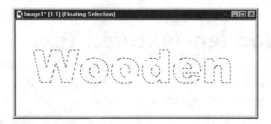

This effect is perfect for your immediate purposes because you will be painting over the text. With the selection marquee around the text, you won't be able to paint outside the lines. This feature would have been great back in the days of the coloring book.

If you need to move the text around, you can do so by moving the mouse pointer over the text until the pointer turns into a four-headed arrow. All you need to do then is click-and-drag the text into position.

It's time to add some texture and color to the text. Follow these steps to do so:

1. Select the Paint Brushes tool.

2. Click the Tools Control tab in the Controls palette and set the Paper Texture to Woodgrain.

3. Click the Brush Tip tab and set the options as follows:

   Shape: Round

   Brush Options: Normal

   Size: 200

   Opacity: 100

   Hardness: 50

   Density: 100

   Step: 25

4. Move the mouse pointer to the left of the text and, while holding down the right mouse button (to paint with the background color instead of the foreground color), sweep the mouse over the text and back again.

You should get a good covering of paint, but not to the point where the grain disappears (see Figure 10.3).

FIGURE 10.3.

Brown woodgrain texture painted onto the text.

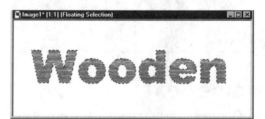

This text already looks good, but the job isn't finished yet.

5. Choose Selections, Modify, Feather; then enter a value of 5 for the number of pixels. This setting expands the selection a little and changes the overall effect.

Feathering a selection not only expands the selection but also softens the edges of the selection. This option can be useful for creating certain effects and for softening the edges of shapes and other objects that you select with the selection tools. I sometimes use this option. To see the difference feathering makes, try following along with an exercise where I use feathering and, at the same time, create the same effect without the feathering option. You can also try using different values for the feathering option to see how they alter the overall effect. In fact, this type of experimenting has resulted in many of the techniques that I use when creating digital images.

A higher feathering value gives you more softness, and a lower value gives you less softness. Play around to see exactly what the effect will be when you change the value.

6. Choose Image, Other, Hot Wax Coating. Adding the Hot Wax Coating brings out the grain, makes the wood texture look a little aged and a bit more realistic and, because of the feathering, adds some definition to the edges of the text.

Your final result should resemble Figure 10.4. Not a bad effect for the amount of work involved.

Creating Chrome Text

Chrome text is one of the most popular effects. I've received many emails asking how to accomplish a chrome effect with different software. The next exercise shows you one way to create this effect in Paint Shop Pro.

Have you ever looked at something that's chrome plated? Not just seen something in chrome, but really looked at it? Take a moment now to step into your kitchen and take a really good look at the faucet fixtures. Go ahead, I'll wait.

What did you see? I'll bet you saw that the fixtures were mostly shades of pale grey (almost, but not quite white), with some darker shades (heading into shades that were almost black) that defined the shape of the fixtures, right?

I discovered a Paint Shop Pro technique that mimics true chrome quite closely. To see how this technique works, open a new 500×200-pixel image with the resolution set to 72 pixels per inch. Then follow these steps:

1. Set the background color to white and the image type to 16.7 million colors.

2. Set the foreground color to white.

3. Select the Text tool and click somewhere in the image to bring up the Add Text dialog box. Enter the following options in the Add Text dialog box:

   Name: Arial Black

   Style: Regular

   Script: Western

   Size: 72

   Text Effects: Antialias

   Alignment: Left

   Place a checkmark in the Floating checkbox.

4. Enter some text and click OK. I, quite naturally, entered the word *Chrome*.

   If the text from the previous exercise or some other session is still visible, just highlight the existing text with the mouse before you enter the new text to replace the old text.

The text should be white on white, and it should be visible only because it's surrounded by the selection marquee (see Figure 10.5).

FIGURE 10.5.

White-on-white text surrounded by the selection marquee.

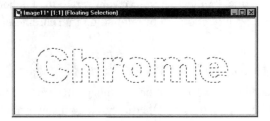

5. Choose Image, Other, Hot Wax Coating.
6. Repeat the process to add another coat of hot wax. You should see your text starting to appear in a light shade of grey (see Figure 10.6).

10

FIGURE 10.6.

A couple of coats of hot wax added to the white-on-white text.

The next step is part of the trick to getting the text to appear as if it is chrome plated.

7. Choose Selections, Modify, Feather; then enter 8 for the value in the number of pixels spin box.
8. Click OK to feather the selection around your text.
9. Apply another coat of hot wax by choosing Image, Other, Hot Wax Coating. Apply a few more coats until your text looks like the text in Figure 10.7.

FIGURE 10.7.

Final chrome text created by manipulating the selection and applying multiple coatings of the Hot Wax filter.

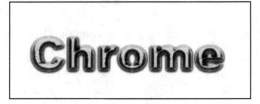

I applied six coatings of hot wax to arrive at the final image you see in Figure 10.7. Two were applied before the feathering and four more after feathering.

If you look at the text and remember your recent trip to the kitchen, I'm sure you'll agree that the effect does a pretty good job of mimicking true chrome plating.

Adding a Drop Shadow

Adding a drop shadow to text used to be a cumbersome process requiring several steps. However, Paint Shop Pro and many other imaging companies have added the capability to add drop shadows to their standard repertoire.

To effectively use the drop shadow filter to create interesting effects with your text, follow these steps:

1. Open a new 500×200-pixel image with the resolution set to 72 pixels per inch. Set the background color to white and the image type to 16.7 million colors.

2. Set the current foreground color to the color you want for your text.

3. Select the Text tool and then click on your image to bring up the Add Text dialog box.

4. Leave most of the settings from the last two exercises, but choose a different font if you'd like. I chose Staccato BT and set the size to 96 points (see Figure 10.8).

FIGURE 10.8.

Text added to a new image and still surrounded by the selection marquee.

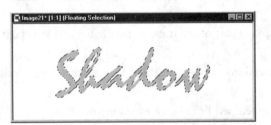

(You may not have this font on your system, but the results you get will be similar regardless of the font you choose.) The selection marquee surrounds the text. Don't deselect the text.

5. Choose Image, Effects, Drop Shadow to open the Drop Shadow dialog box (see Figure 10.9).

6. Choose the color for the shadow from the Color pull-down menu at the top of the Drop Shadow dialog box. The choices are Foreground Color, Background Color, White, Black, Red Green, and Blue.

FIGURE 10.9.

The Drop Shadow dialog box.

If you need a color other than white, black, red, green, or blue, simply set the foreground or background color before choosing the Drop Shadow effect.

7. To arrive at the image in Figure 10.10, set the options in the Drop Shadow dialog box as follows: Color is Black, Opacity is 50, Blur is 5, Vertical Offset is 11, and Horizontal Offset is 8.

FIGURE 10.10.

Drop Shadow added to text.

You can use drop shadows to give the appearance of depth to your text. A closer, darker, sharper-edged shadow (as shown in Figure 10.11) gives the appearance of the text being just slightly above the screen (or printed page).

FIGURE 10.11.

Sharp-edged, dark drop shadow added to text.

To achieve the hard-edged, close shadow, I used the following values:

Opacity: 80

Blur: 3

Vertical Offset: 7

Horizontal Offset: 5

The following values produced the drop shadow effect in Figure 10.12:

Opacity: 60

Blur: 15

Vertical Offset: 15

Horizontal Offset: 11

FIGURE 10.12.

Softer-edged, lighter drop shadow added to text.

Note how the text appears to hover higher in Figure 10.12 than it does in Figure 10.11. This effect is due to the softness and different offsets of the shadow in Figure 10.12.

You should experiment with the various settings in the Drop Shadow dialog box to see how they affect the appearance of your text.

Adding a Glow to Your Text

With the popularity of the television show *The X-Files*, people have been asking how to create the glowing text effect seen in the opening credits.

The following exercise shows you how to create the glow. Follows these steps:

1. Open a new 500×200-pixel image with the resolution set to 72 pixels per inch. Set the background color to black and the image type to 16.7 million colors.

2. Set the current foreground color to a bright green (I used R: 30, G: 255, and B: 45) and the current background color to black.

3. Select the Text tool and click in the image to bring up the Add Text dialog box.

4. Use the settings from the previous exercise and choose a font that resembles a typewriter font. I chose Times New Roman (see Figure 10.13).

FIGURE 10.13.

Bright green text on black.

5. Choose Selections, Select None to deselect the text (or you can right-click on the image when the Selection tool is selected).

6. Choose Image, Blur, Gaussian Blur; then set Radius to 5.00. Click OK.

7. Apply the Gaussian Blur one more time with the same settings. The text should now have very soft edges and be blurry (see Figure 10.14).

FIGURE 10.14.

Bright green text on black blurred with two applications of the Gaussian Blur filter.

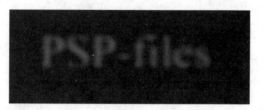

10

8. Swap the foreground and background colors by clicking on the small, bent, two-headed arrow icon to the lower-left of the foreground/background color swatches in the Color palette.

9. Click in the image again to bring up the Add Text dialog box. To add the same text, just click OK.

10. The text comes into the image in black this time. All that you need to do is position it over the blurry green text from the preceding steps.

    To move the text into place, move the mouse pointer over the text until the four-headed arrow cursor appears and click-and-drag the black text into place over the green text.

11. Choose Selections, Select None to remove the marquee, and you should end up with text that resembles Figure 10.15.

FIGURE 10.15.

Final glowing, X-Files–type text.

Paint Shop Pro can produce a nearly unlimited number of text effects. All you need to do is play around, try new things, apply filters, and have some fun.

There are probably enough text effects to be the subject of a whole book. We've still got plenty of other topics to cover, however.

To learn a few more text effects, visit my web site at http://www.grafx-design.com. You'll find some other text effects along with some more advanced Paint Shop Pro techniques.

Summary

In this hour you learned how to enter text with the Text tool. As well, you learned how to create some cool effects, including wooden textures, chrome, and drop shadows, using Paint Shop Pro options.

At this point, it's time to start covering some more advanced topics, the first of which is layers.

Workshop

The workshop contains a question and answer section to help answer the most commonly asked questions and quiz questions to help you solidify your understanding of the material covered.

Q&A

Q Can I use some of the filters, such as the Drop Shadow filter, on objects other than text?

A Yes, you can use all the various filters and effects in Paint Shop Pro on virtually any object you create. Some filters require you to make a selection first. To review how selections work, flip back to Hour 5, "Creating and Working with Selections."

Q How can I enter text in the current background color?

A The Text tool doesn't work the same way that other tools work in that you can't right-click to enter text in the background color. Instead, you should temporarily swap the foreground and background colors by clicking the small, bent, two-headed arrow icon to the lower left of the foreground/background color swatches in the Color palette. You can then enter the text with the color you've set and swap the colors back when you're done.

Q I don't seem to have the same fonts as you do. Why not?

A Paint Shop Pro uses the fonts installed on your system. Many products, both software and hardware, ship with packages of fonts these days. It's quite possible that you have some fonts that I don't have, as well. If I use a certain font that you don't have, hunt through the ones you do have until you find something that comes close.

Quiz

1. How can you enter text in a larger point size than the predefined 72 points?
2. How can you make text appear to float higher off the screen?
3. Why would you want to apply a filter more than once?
4. Why would you need to set the alignment of text in the Add Text dialog box?

Answers

1. You can enter the value manually in the window above the predefined values in the Add Text dialog box.
2. You can use drop shadows to make the text appear to float higher or lower, depending on the edge hardness and offset of the shadow. Text appears higher as you soften the shadow and enter larger numbers for the offsets.
3. Multiple applications of a particular filter can result in spectacular results that wouldn't be possible otherwise. Playing with filters and learning how they work, even in multiple applications, will make your work stand out from the crowd.
4. The Alignment option is useful only when you enter more than one line of text—this option aligns all the lines of text.

10

PART III
Tools to Work Efficiently

Hour

Hour 11

Layers

This hour introduces the following issues about using layers:

- Understanding layers
- Using the Layers palette
- Using the Layers menu
- Using layers effectively
- Understanding the blending modes

Layers are a powerful new addition to Paint Shop Pro 5. Layers enable you to do much more with Paint Shop Pro than was possible with earlier versions. The first thing that struck me when I first ran version 5 was my ability to use layers. Layers are such a powerful tool that after you learn how to harness their power, you'll wonder how you ever got by without them.

Understanding Layers

You can think of *layers* as separate drawing surfaces that lay on top of one another in Paint Shop Pro, much like sheets of paper in a sketchbook (see Figure 11.1).

FIGURE 11.1.

The concept of layers.

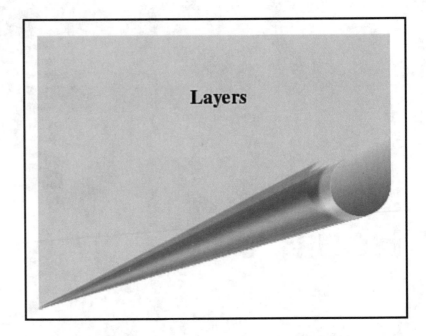

Layers are quite similar to sheets of paper, yet they perform many additional functions. Imagine having a digital sketchbook and being able to see each layer through the others above it. Further, imagine being able to move or edit the objects on any given layer without disturbing the other objects on other layers.

Now what if you could blend the different layers in ways that enable you to selectively see portions of one layer through another. This description suggests just how powerful layers are.

All of that power is hidden behind a relatively easy interface. The interface I'm talking about is the Layers palette (see Figure 11.2).

FIGURE 11.2.

The Layers palette.

Figure 11.2 shows the Layers palette for an image that has two layers: the background layer and another layer, Layer1, above the background layer.

Each image that you open in Paint Shop Pro has at least one layer, regardless of the file format, which is called the background layer. You can, and I think you should, add subsequent layers as you work on an image. I discuss why you should do so as I progress through the remainder of this hour.

The Layers Palette Dissected

If you take another look at Figure 11.2, you'll see the various parts of a layer that you can adjust.

From the left, you can see a layer's name. The current layer seems to be indented. You can name layers anything you want. If you're working on a simple image, naming the layers may not be necessary. However, when you get to working on an image with more than four or five layers, giving descriptive names to the layers helps to keep things organized.

When you add a layer, you have the option of naming it. If you choose not to name the new layer, Paint Shop Pro assigns a generic name such as Layer1, Layer2, and so on. If you decide to name a layer after you've created it, you can do so. Simply click on the layer's name in the Layers palette to bring up the Layers Properties dialog box. You can enter the name for your layer there.

You can see a thumbnail view of a layer's contents by holding the mouse pointer over the layer's name in the Layers palette. The small thumbnail view appears at the lower left of the Layers palette as a small, floating window.

Next to the name is the Visibility Toggle button. You can use this button to turn the layer on and off. This feature can be a big help when you're positioning other layers and when you're trying to see what effect one layer has on the others.

Next in line is the Protect Transparency Toggle button. You can use this button to protect transparent areas on a layer from changes that you make with drawing and painting tools.

The next button is the Layer Group Toggle button. This button normally contains a small asterisk. As you group layers together, though, the layers share a group number that replaces the asterisk on the buttons for those layers. You can use this button to group layers together. I describe how to use this option later in this hour.

The slider bar in the middle of the palette controls the opacity of a layer. You can use the slider to set the level of opacity of a layer. When you slide the button to the left, the layer gets more and more transparent, thus allowing the layers beneath it to show through.

Beside the Opacity slider, you have the Layer Blend Mode pull-down menu. You can select from a variety of blending modes. Changing the blending modes of a layer enables

11

you to perform feats of great magic. You see evidence of some of this magic later in this hour and in other upcoming hours, as well.

The second to last button is the Enable Layer Mask Toggle button. This button enables you to turn on and off a layer mask.

Last you have the Link Mask Toggle button. This button enables you to link a layer mask to the layer so that, when you move an object on a layer, the mask follows it. I describe masks in more depth in Hour 12, "Masks."

At the bottom-left corner of the Layers palette, you'll find the Add New Layer (a blank page) and Delete Layer (a trashcan) icons.

You can add a new layer simply by clicking on the Add New Layer icon. Also, you can duplicate an existing layer by clicking-and-dragging the layer's name onto the icon.

You can delete the current layer by clicking the Delete Layer icon; you can delete specific layers by dragging-and-dropping the layer's name onto the icon.

The Layers Menu Dissected

Many layer options are available to you via the Layers menu. The following menu choices are available:

- The New menu creates a new layer exactly as the Add New Layer icon does.
- The Duplicate menu duplicates the current layer. This item has the same effect as dragging-and-dropping a layer onto the Add New Layer icon.
- The Delete menu deletes the current layer. The difference between the menu command and dragging the layer onto the small trashcan icon is that the menu option doesn't ask you to verify the operation.
- The Properties menu brings up the Layers Properties dialog box.
- The Matting menu has a submenu. You can use this option to remove black or white fringes from the edges of objects on a layer. These edges can come from anti-aliasing.
- The Arrange menu enables you to arrange the order of the layers that make up your image.
- The View menu enables you to view all layers or only the current layer. This menu is a great shortcut for viewing a single layer when you're working on a multilayer image.
- The Merge menu option enables you to merge all visible layers or flatten the image. Flattening the image converts a multilayer image into an image with one layer.

Using Layers Effectively

Now that you've had a look at the Layers palette, it's time to play around with, and get used to, layers themselves. Follow these steps to do so:

1. Open a new image at 500×500 pixels with the resolution set to 72 pixels per inch, the background color set to white, and the image type set to 16.7 million colors.

2. Set the foreground color to black.

3. Select the Text tool. In the Add Text dialog box, choose a large font and type the letter **B** for background. Click OK.

4. Move the letter to the upper-left corner of the image and choose Selections, Select None. I set the size to 150 and used Arial Black for the font (see Figure 11.3).

FIGURE 11.3.

Some text on the background layer.

11

5. Now add a new layer by clicking the Add New Layer icon at the lower-left corner of the Layers palette. (The Add New Layer icon looks like a blank page.)

6. When the Layer Properties dialog box pops up (see Figure 11.4), click OK to accept the defaults.

   Most of the options in this dialog box can be set from the Layers palette and were discussed previously in this hour. The blend ranges option is discussed in more detail in the upcoming section "Understanding the Blending Modes."

7. Select the Text tool again and enter the number 1.

8. Move the 1 into the lower-left corner of the image (see Figure 11.5).

FIGURE 11.4.

Layer Properties dialog box.

FIGURE 11.5.

A new layer containing a 1 is added.

9. Repeat the process of adding a new layer; this time add the number 2 to the new layer. Move the 2 into the upper-right corner of the image.

10. Add one last layer and add the number 3 to it. (You should end up with four layers: the background, Layer1, Layer2, and Layer3.)

11. Move the 3 to the lower-right corner of the image and choose Selections, Select None.

You should have an image that resembles the one shown in Figure 11.6.

FIGURE 11.6.

Four layers with text and numbers.

Moving Layers

Hmmm. There seems to be a problem with the order of the numbers, though. The 1 and the 2 are in the wrong place and should be switched.

If you had created this image in an older version of Paint Shop Pro, you'd pretty much have to start over. There would be no easy way to change the placement of the numbers. With layers, though, the process is easy.

To see how easy, select the Mover tool (it's the four-headed arrow icon and is the fifth one down in the Tool palette) and then follow these steps:

1. Click on the Layer2 button in the Layers palette and click-and-drag the 2 down to the lower-left corner of the image. Don't worry about it covering the number 1. Because the numbers are on different layers, it really doesn't matter.

2. Click the Layer1 button in the Layers palette and click-and-drag the number 1 to the upper-right corner.

Notice how only the number 1 moved even though it appeared to be covered by the number 2. Again, this trick is possible because the numbers are on different layers. The numbers seem to be in a better order now (see Figure 11.7).

Grouping Layers Together

What if you needed to move two or more layers as though they were a single layer? That's where the Layer Group Toggle button comes in (recall that it's the button with the asterisk on it on the Layers dialog box).

11

FIGURE 11.7.

*Four layers with text
and numbers in a
better order.*

To move the number 3 and the number 1 together, click the Layer Group Toggle button for both layers. The small asterisk on each button should turn to a 1, signifying that the two layers are now grouped together as group 1. If you use the Mover tool now, both the 1 and the 3 move together.

You can create different groups with different layers. You can also toggle back to where the layers are all ungrouped by repeatedly clicking the Layer Group Toggle button for any of the layers.

Changing the Opacity and Visibility Options

Let's have some more fun. Try these steps:

1. Drag-and-drop Layer3 onto the Delete Layer icon (the small trashcan icon at the bottom-left side of the Layers palette).

2. Paint Shop Pro, through a dialog box, asks you to verify that you want to delete the layer. Click Yes.

3. Change the foreground color to something other than black or white. A really bright red or a pale blue might be nice.

4. Add another new layer and add the number 3 to it via the Text tool.

5. Choose Selections, Select None to remove the selection marquee from around the number.

6. Move the number 3 over the number 1 (use the Mover tool). Note how the 3 completely covers the number 1.

7. Drag the Opacity slider for Layer3 to the left and watch the image as you do so. You should notice the number 3 getting fainter and allowing the number 1 to show through (see Figure 11.8).

FIGURE 11.8.

Adjusting the opacity of one of the layers to allow another, lower layer to show through.

Amazing! What feats of magic!

Now click the Layer Visibility Toggle button (the first icon to the right of the layer's name, with a small red, green, and blue square) for Layer3. Whoa! The number 3 has disappeared.

You can bring it right back, though, by clicking the Layer Visibility Toggle button once more. Wow, more magic!

Bring the opacity of Layer3 back to 100 so that the 3 covers the 1 again. Now click-and-drag the Layer3 icon from its position at the top of the Layers palette (see Figure 11.9) so that it's below Layer1 (see Figure 11.10).

Now the 1 is covering the 3. This change is due to the reordering of the layers.

It's like magic! But wait, there's more! Next you learn all about the use of blending modes within layers.

11

FIGURE 11.9.

The original layers in the order in which they were created.

FIGURE 11.10.

The layers with their order rearranged.

Understanding the Blending Modes

The blending modes enable you to blend layers together in weird and wonderful ways.

Just as you've seen how you can change the opacity of a layer so that the layer(s) below shows through, you can change how layers interact with each other. The blending modes in the Layers palette control the blending function.

Several blending modes are available, and they combine layers in different ways. I could, as some books do, simply show you a couple of images stored on two layers and then show you how the different modes affect the image. This approach wouldn't work too well in black and white, though, and you really wouldn't learn anything from the demonstration. Instead, I'll describe the modes and then show you a cool effect you can create with one of the blending modes.

You can access the various layer-blending modes by clicking the pull-down menu for each layer in the Layers palette.

The available blending modes and their effects are as follows:

- Normal—Blends the modes only with the Opacity slider in the Layers palette.
- Darken—Pixels in the current layer that are darker than the pixels in the underlying layer are applied while lighter pixels disappear.
- Lighten—Pixels in the current layer that are lighter than the pixels in the underlying image are applied while darker pixels disappear.
- Hue—Applies the hue of the current layer to the pixels in the underlying layers.
- Saturation—Applies the saturation of the current layer to the pixels in the underlying layers.
- Color—Applies the hue and saturation of the current layer to the pixels of the underlying layers. This mode does not affect the luminance of the pixels in the underlying layers.
- Luminance—Applies the luminance values in the current layer to the pixels in the underlying layers.
- Multiply—Combines the color of the pixels in the current layer with the color of the pixels of the underlying layers to produce a darker color. Multiplying any color with black leaves results in black, whereas multiplying any color with white leaves the color unchanged.
- Screen—Is the opposite of Multiply in that the pixels combine to form lighter colors.
- Dissolve—Randomly replaces some of the pixels in the current layer with those from underlying layers. This mode creates a sparkle effect.
- Overlay—Preserves patterns or color in the current layer while allowing the highlights and shadows from the underlying layer to show through.
- Hard Light—Adds highlights or shadows but is a little harsher than the Overlay mode.
- Soft Light—Adds softer highlights and shadows than the Overlay and Hard Light modes.
- Difference—Subtracts the current layer's color from the color of the underlying layers, depending on which is lighter.
- Dodge—Lightens underlying layers using the current layer's pixel lightness values.
- Burn—Darkens underlying layers using the current layer's pixel lightness values.
- Exclusion—Creates an effect similar to the Difference mode, but softer.

11

To see the effects these blending modes have, follow these steps:

1. Open two images and copy the first one as a new layer in the second. To do so, choose Selections, Select All. Then choose Edit, Copy.

2. Make the second image current by clicking its title bar and then choose Edit, Paste as New Layer.

3. With the two images combined as one with two layers, cycle through the blending modes to see the effect each has on the image.

4. To see how you can put the blending modes to real-world use, create a new image at 500×500 pixels with the resolution set to 72 pixels per inch, the background color set to white, and the image type set to 16.7 million colors.

5. Set the foreground color to a medium brown. I used R: 195, G: 154, B: 11.

6. Select the Paint Brushes tool and set the Paper Texture to Woodgrain. Set the Paint Brushes options as follows:

   Shape: Round

   Brush Options: Normal

   Size: 200

   Opacity: 100

   Hardness: 50

   Density: 100

   Step: 25

7. Sweep the paintbrush back and forth over the image to get a nice, dark, woodgrain texture.

8. Set the foreground color to white and choose Image, Other, Hot Wax Coating to give the grain more depth (see Figure 11.11).

9. Add a new layer by clicking the Add New Layer icon in the Layers palette.

10. Fill the new layer with white using the Flood Fill tool.

11. Change the foreground color to black.

12. Select the Text tool and add a large @ (at sign) to the layer. I set the font size to 300.

13. Choose Selections, Select None.

14. Emboss the text by choosing Image, Other Emboss.

15. Blur the embossed text by choosing Image, Blur, Gaussian Blur and using a value of 2.00. The upper layer should resemble Figure 11.12.

FIGURE 11.11.

Background layer filled with a woodgrain texture.

FIGURE 11.12.

Upper layer containing embossed, blurred text.

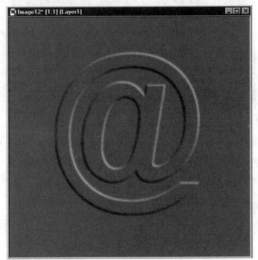

11

16. Set the blending mode of the top layer (the one with the embossed, blurred text) to Hard Light.

Wow! Even more magic (see Figure 11.13).

The Hard Light blending mode allows the highlights and shadows to show through, yet the woodgrain texture is preserved. You should take the time to play around with the various blending modes to see how they affect the layers that make up your image.

FIGURE 11.13.

*The two layers com-
bined with the Hard
Light mode yield a
nice woodcut image.*

The great part about the changes that the blending modes create is that they aren't permanent (unless you flatten the layers). You can always go back and try another blending
mode. In fact, try setting the blending mode of the image you just created to Soft Light
or Overlay. See the difference?

I use layers a lot more throughout the rest of this book—so much so, that you'll be an
expert with layers by the time you work through the remaining hours.

Summary

In this hour you learned about layers. You learned to create and delete layers. You saw
how easy it is to move objects around when they're on a separate layer. You saw how the
opacity feature works and how to change the order of the layers in an image. Finally, you
saw firsthand how blending modes work.

I believe that you're ready to see how masks work. I cover them in the next hour.

Workshop

The workshop contains a question and answer section to help answer the most commonly asked questions and quiz questions to help you solidify your understanding of the material covered.

Q&A

Q I've added a layer and placed an object on it, but now I don't want the layer any more. What can I do?

A You can delete any layer by making it current and then clicking the Delete Layer icon. You can also drag-and-drop the layer onto the Delete Layer icon or choose Layers, Delete.

Q I want to change the order of the layers in my image. How do I do so?

A You can drag-and-drop layers to change the layer order. You can also use the Layers, Arrange option to change the order of your layers.

Q I'd like to be able to see an underlying layer through one that's on top of it. Is this possible?

A Yes. You can change the opacity of any layer by moving the Opacity slider. Doing so will enable you to see underlying layers through the layer whose opacity you've adjusted.

Quiz

1. How do you move two or more layers as though they were one?
2. How do you toggle off a layer's visibility?
3. How do you combine two or more layers into one?
4. How do you create a new layer?
5. How do you duplicate a layer?

Answers

1. You can group layers together using the Layer Group Toggle button on the Layers palette.
2. You can use the Layer Visibility Toggle button on the Layers palette to toggle a layer on and off.
3. You can combine two or more layers by making them visible (and all others invisible) and choosing Layers, Merge, Merge Visible. You can also flatten the image, essentially merging all layers, by choosing Layers, Merge, Merge All (Flatten).

11

4. You can click the Add New Layer icon, or you can choose Layers, New.

5. You can drag-and-drop a layer onto the Add New Layer icon, or you can choose Layers, Duplicate.

Hour **12**

Masks

This hour introduces the following issues about Paint Shop Pro masks:

- Understanding what masks are and what they do
- Using the Masks menus
- Creating your first mask
- Creating a more complex mask
- Delving into advanced mask topics

Masks, unlike layers, are not new to Paint Shop Pro version 5. Masks were available in previous versions, but this feature is now more powerful. Mastery of masks and masking techniques marks the difference, I believe, between a causal user and the accomplished one. After working your way through this hour, you'll certainly be a more accomplished Paint Shop Pro user.

In this hour, I show you what masks are and how they can be used. As well, I show you several examples of the digital magic that masks can help you create.

What Are Masks?

Masks are greyscale images that work with existing layers. They enable you to create special effects that would be difficult, or even impossible, to create otherwise.

Masks are analogous to masking tape, but they are far more powerful. If you've done any painting around the house, you probably used masking tape to mask off doorframes and windows. This procedure is similar to what you would do with masks in Paint Shop Pro.

Masks enable you to control how the changes you make affect your image.

Because masks are greyscale, you can save them in alpha channels. This feature enables you to save a mask along with your image so that you can use the same mask in later sessions. Recall that *alpha channels* are areas where you can store selections. These alpha channels are stored with an image if you save the image in PSP, TIF, or TGA format.

Masks can also be saved separately and loaded into the same image in a later session or used with other images. Because masks are, in their own right, images, you can edit them using any of the painting and drawing tools in Paint Shop Pro.

Masks enable you to "mask out" areas of images. These areas can then be selected and removed from the image to be placed into another, for example.

You can use masks to blend objects on one layer with objects on other layers in ways that you might see in magazine ads and product brochures. These are just some of the ways that professionals use masks to their advantage.

The Masks Menu

The Masks menu (see Figure 12.1) contains all the options you need to access your masks.

FIGURE 12.1.

The Masks menu.

From within the Masks menu, you can create a new mask, delete an existing mask, invert a mask, edit a mask, and view a layer's mask. You can also load a mask from disk or an alpha channel as well as save a mask to disk or an alpha channel.

Because masks are similar to selections, they can be saved (and loaded) in much the same way that selections can. You can save masks as separate files or in alpha channels. Saving a mask as an alpha channel has the advantage that the mask remains with the image that it was created for.

When you choose the New option, you get a submenu that enables you to create the new mask and either show all or hide all. You can also create the mask from a selection, choosing to show all or hide all of the selection. Finally, you can create the mask from an image. This option enables you to create a mask from any image that you have open in Paint Shop Pro.

Creating Your First Mask

Recall that masks allow changes to show through where the mask is black and block changes from occurring where the mask is white.

However, because masks are greyscale, the changes can show up partially in an image where the mask is grey rather than black or white. If the mask is a lighter grey, the changes will be less visible. Where the mask is a darker grey, the changes will be more evident.

To get a feeling for how masks work, you can create a new mask. Follow these steps to create an image with a simple mask:

1. Open a new image at 500×200 pixels with the resolution set to 72 pixels per inch, the background color set to white, and the image type set to 16.7 million colors.

2. Create a new layer by clicking the Add New Layer button at the bottom of the Layers palette. You can open the Layers palette (if it's not already visible on your screen) by clicking on the Toggle Layer Palette button in the toolbar.

3. Set the foreground color to blue: Either click in the foreground color swatch and set the color or choose the color from the color picker. You can choose any shade of blue, or another color altogether, for this demonstration.

4. Use the Text tool to enter some text. I entered the word **Mask** in 100-point, bold, Arial Black (see Figure 12.2).

5. Choose Selections, Select None to deselect the text.

12

Figure 12.2.

*Text entered with the
Text tool.*

6. Choose Masks, New, Show All to create a new mask. However, you won't see any changes to the image at this point.

7. Choose Masks, View Mask. You still won't see any changes because you chose Show All. With the Show All option, the mask is completely white, and no changes to your image occur. (*Show All* refers to showing the image—or more specifically to showing the image through the mask, in effect creating a totally white mask— not the mask.)

8. Choose Masks, Edit. Now any changes you make to the current level affect the mask, rather than the object(s) on the layer.

9. Choose the Selection tool and set the Selection Type to Rectangle in the Controls palette.

10. Draw a rectangular selection that encompasses the top third of the image.

11. Select the Flood Fill tool.

12. Set the foreground color to black and click in the selection to fill it with black.

Whoa! What happened there? The selection was filled, all right, but it wasn't filled with black. It was filled with a reddish color, right? What you're seeing is the mask itself. You're seeing the mask because you've toggled on the View Masks option. You can also tell that you're viewing the mask and the image through the mask because the word (*MASK*) appears on the image's title bar.

To turn off the view of the mask, choose Masks, View Mask. Hey! What happened this time? The mask has disappeared but so has the top third of the text. The text hasn't really disappeared; rather it has been "masked out" and is now invisible. Now follow these steps:

1. Select the Selection tool again and draw another selection that encompasses the middle third of the image. You may have to click the Selection tool outside of the currently selected area first.

2. Set the foreground color to a medium grey.

3. Select the Flood Fill tool again and fill the selected area with grey.

Okay, okay, what's going on here? The grey color doesn't show up and this time the text seems to fade out to a pale blue (or a paler version of the color you used for the text—see Figure 12.3).

FIGURE 12.3.

Text masked off with black, grey, and white.

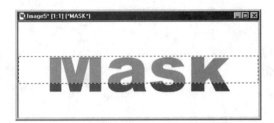

To see how the mask looks now, choose Masks, View Mask again.

Now the top third is filled with red; the middle third is red, but you can see the text through it; and the lower third is not red at all, and the text is completely visible.

This step proves my earlier explanation about how the black portion of a mask allows the lower layer to show through completely, the grey portion allows some of the lower layer to show through, and the white portion of a mask allows none of the lower layer to show through.

Now you may be asking, "What exactly is showing through?" You may also wonder why I didn't just color the text this way instead of going through all of the work of creating the masks.

Well, it's true that this text could have been created in a much easier fashion if you look at just the text on white. But what if the text was on a textured layer?

If the text was on a separate layer above a textured layer, you'd be able to see the texture through the text; this effect could not be easily re-created without using masks.

To see how the mask would work with the text and a textured background, it's time to create a more complex mask.

Creating a More Complex Mask

Open a new image at 500×200 pixels with the resolution set to 72 pixels per inch, the background color set to white, and the image type set to 16.7 million colors. Then follow these steps:

1. Set the foreground color to a pale yellow. I used R: 239, G: 244, B: 164.

12

2. Select the Paint Brushes tool and set the options as follows:

   Paper Texture: Woodgrain

   Shape: Round

   Brush Tip: Normal

   Size: 200

   Opacity: 100

   Hardness: 50

   Density: 100

   Step: 25

3. Draw the paintbrush back and forth across the image a couple of times to get a good texture.

4. Choose Image, Other, Hot Wax Coating to apply a hot wax coating and increase the woodgrain texture.

5. Add a new layer by clicking the Add New Layer icon at the bottom of the Layers palette.

6. Set the foreground color to black.

7. Select the Text tool and add some large text to the image. I used 100-point, bold, Arial Black and entered the word **Mask** (see Figure 12.4).

FIGURE 12.4.

Black text on a separate layer above a woodgrain texture.

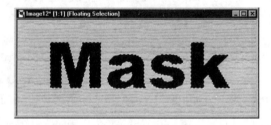

8. Choose Selections, Defloat. This setting drops the text, but leaves it selected.

9. Choose Masks, New, Hide Selection. The text seems to disappear and the selection marquee is visible over the texture background.

   If you choose Masks, View Mask, you'll see that the mask is covering the text with a partially transparent red color.

10. Set the foreground color to black and the background color to white.

11. Choose Masks, Edit so that you'll be painting on the mask and not on the actual image.

12. Select the Flood Fill tool.

13. In the Controls palette, set the Fill Style to Linear Gradient.

14. Click the Options button and set the Direction to 180 degrees.

15. Click each letter to fill its mask with the gradient.

16. If the View Mask option is still on, toggle it off by choosing Masks, View Mask.

Your final image should resemble Figure 12.5.

FIGURE 12.5.

Black text masked with a linear gradient to allow the textured layer below to show through.

An effect such as this would be almost impossible to accomplish without the use of a mask.

You could have text on a layer above the texture and adjust its opacity, but that would affect all of the text. What you've done here is use a gradient mask to allow the text to gradually blend into the texture.

Saving and Loading Masks

You can save and load your masks after you've created them. Masks such as the two you created in the previous exercises are not hard to re-create, and you probably wouldn't need to save them. If you spend more than a few minutes creating a mask, though, you'll probably want to save it.

To save a mask, simply choose Masks, Save to Disk or choose Masks, Save to Alpha Channel. Saving the mask to disk saves the mask separately; saving it to an alpha channel saves the mask along with your image.

If you save your mask as an alpha channel, though, you'll need to save your image in PSP, TIF, or TGA format to preserve the channel.

If you choose to save the mask to disk, you'll be prompted for a filename. Leave the default extension .msk so that Paint Shop Pro will recognize the file when you decide, at a later date, to load the mask.

12

Understanding Advanced Mask Topics

In the last exercise, you saw that masks can be made from selections. The reverse is also true. You can create selections from masks.

Because you can use the drawing and painting tools to create a mask, you can create very complex masks. When you finish "painting" your mask, you can create a selection from it.

What can you do with this complex mask/selection? Digital magic!

How you ever wondered how to isolate someone from an image? Have you ever thought that it might be fun to cut someone from one image and place him or her into another? These effects, and more, are possible with the following technique.

For this exercise, I need some help from my assistant, Zoë (see Figure 12.6).

FIGURE 12.6.

Zoë on her blankie.

My niece, Zoë, was just under a year old when this photo was taken, but her mom said she could help with this lesson. You won't have this particular photo, so you load one of your own photos from which you want to remove an object, or person. Then follow these steps:

If you don't have access to an image to try this exercise with, load the Guitar.psp file from the Paint Shop Pro CD-ROM. This image is multilayered, though, so you may need to flatten it to have all of the steps in the exercise work properly.

1. Create a new layer by clicking the Add New Layer icon at the bottom of the Layers palette.

2. Fill the new layer with white and drag it down so that it's below the layer with the photo on it.

> If you have trouble dragging the new layer below the layer with your photo on it because the photo layer is the "background" layer, you can double-click the background layer and accept the defaults in the Layer Properties dialog box. Doing so will promote the background to a layer and enable you to rearrange the layers.

3. Choose Masks, New, Hide All.

4. Choose Masks, Edit.

5. Choose Masks, View Mask. You should see your photo behind the red mask (see Figure 12.7).

FIGURE 12.7.

Zoë with the full mask in place.

12

6. Set the foreground color to black and the background color to white. (Either click in the foreground/background color swatches and set the colors or choose the colors from the color picker.)

7. Now you're ready to start working on the mask. Select the Paint Brushes tool and set the options to the following:

Brush Type: Normal

Size: 5

Shape: Round

Paper Texture: None

You may want to zoom in a little (see Figure 12.8), and you'll probably want to change the brush size from time to time.

FIGURE 12.8.

Zoë with some of the mask removed.

8. The goal here is to remove the red masked area from the portion of the photo that you want to select. I want to select Zoë and leave out the blanket. Painting or drawing with white removes the mask; painting or drawing with black replaces it. Because you can replace the mask, it doesn't matter if you draw outside the lines, as it were. Try to come as close as possible, though, so that there'll be a smooth transition from the object to its new background.

If you make a mistake, swap the foreground and background colors by clicking on the small, bent, two-headed arrow icon below the current foreground/background colors swatch. You can go back and forth like this removing and replacing the mask until you've removed the mask completely from the object you want to select (see Figure 12.9).

FIGURE 12.9.

Zoë with completed mask.

9. You can create the selection from the completed mask by choosing Selections, From Mask. Doing so creates a selection from the mask you just "painted" (see Figure 12.10).

FIGURE 12.10.

Selection created from finished mask.

12

You should now have a selection that exactly matches the object or person you want to copy.

10. Choose Masks, View Mask to toggle off the mask, and you'll see that the object you masked out is selected.

11. Choose Edit, Copy.

12. Open the new image you want to paste the selected object, or person, into. I created an image of clouds to depict what a little angel my niece is.

13. With the new image active, choose Edit, Paste as Layer and move the selection into place (see Figure 12.11).

FIGURE 12.11.

Zoë in the clouds.

That's it! There's much more digital magic that you can accomplish with masks. I use masks again later in the book when I discuss composites in Hour 19, "Compositing."

Summary

In this hour, you've discovered masks. Masks are images that work with existing layers and enable you to create special effects that are otherwise difficult or impossible to do. You've learned how to create simple and complex masks and how to save and load masks. You've seen how masks do their magic. The best way to become more comfortable with masks is to play around and practice using them. They are worth the time and effort!

I believe that you're ready to learn about channels and see how they work. I cover them in the next hour.

Workshop

The workshop contains a question and answer section to help answer the most commonly asked questions and quiz questions to help you solidify your understanding of the material covered.

Q&A

Q Why can't I see the new mask I added?

A You must choose Masks, View Mask to see the current mask.

Q I tried to change the mask, but I changed the image instead. Why?

A You must choose Masks, Edit to edit the mask instead of the image.

Q When I add a mask and choose Masks, Edit, I can't set any colors other than black, white, and shades of grey. How come?

A The reason you can use only black, white, and shades of grey when working on a mask is that masks are greyscale and, therefore, cannot contain any color information.

Quiz

1. How do you create a new mask from a selection?

2. How many colors can you use to "paint" a mask?

3. How do you delete a mask?

4. How can you save a mask?

5. If you create a mask from an object and decide to move the object, can the mask follow the object as you move it? (This is a trick question, and the answer depends on your remembering what you learned about the Layers palette in Hour 11, "Layers.")

Answers

1. After creating the selection, you can create a mask from it by choosing Masks, New, Hide Selection or by choosing Masks, New, Show Selection.

2. Technically, none (masks are greyscale). You can use black, white, and all the shades of grey, though, for a total of 256 colors.

3. You can delete a mask by choosing Masks, Delete. You'll be asked if you want to merge the mask into the current layer. You should select no to delete the mask.

4. You can save a mask by choosing Masks, Save to Disk or by choosing Mask, Save to Alpha Channel.

5. Yes, the layer can be linked to the mask via the Link Mask Toggle button in the Layers palette. When you link the mask to the layer, the mask moves with the object (if you move the object with the Mover tool), keeping the object properly masked.

12

HOUR 13

Channels

This hour introduces the following issues about understanding and using channels:

- Understanding what channels are and how they are used
- Splitting and combining channels
- Identifying information in channels
- Making channels work for you

Channels, unlike layers, are not new to Paint Shop Pro version 5. Channels have been available in previous versions. Like layers and masks, channels are quite mysterious and powerful.

In this hour, I show you what channels are and how they can be used.

What Are Channels?

Every image you create, whether it's layered or not, whether it's 16.7 million colors or greyscale, can be broken down into its component channels. How an image breaks down into channels depends on how you want to use the channels. If you want to use the channels to create color separations so that a service bureau can print your image, for example, you need to split your image into C, M, Y, and K channels.

Essentially, *channels* are greyscale representations of the information that makes up each image. Each greyscale channel holds part of the information that makes up an image.

If, for example, you split an image into its red, green, and blue components, the Red channel will contain the red information in the original image. Likewise, the Green channel will hold the green information, and the Blue channel will hold the blue information.

Splitting Channels

Note that splitting an image into channels does not affect the original image. Splitting an image into channels creates completely new images—one for each channel. Even recombining these images (or channels) into an image doesn't affect the original.

You split the channels of an image when you want to work on separate channels of an image, for example an image that you took with a digital camera. Sometimes digital cameras don't do a great job, and the resulting photos need some corrections.

A way to correct the problems inherent with images taken with a charged couple device (CCD) is to examine each channel. The Blue channel is usually the biggest culprit, and fixing the Blue channel (sometimes with just a little softening) and recombining the channels into an RGB image helps tremendously.

Splitting (and combining) channels in Paint Shop Pro is easy. To split an image into its separate channels, simply choose Colors, Channel Splitting and then choose the type of channels you want to split the image into. You can choose from RGB, HSL, and CMYK.

Do these acronyms look familiar? They should. These are the different ways you have of looking at the colors that make up your images in Paint Shop Pro.

For the most part, you can ignore the CMYK format. This format is most useful when you need color separations for high-end printing. The subject of color separations is beyond the scope of this book. If you plan on doing lots of high-end printing, you should consult with the personnel at your local service bureau.

Ignoring the CMYK leaves you with two choices, RGB and HSL. Which one is best for a specific use depends on many factors, including what exactly you'll be using the channels for. In the following sections, I explain how to use channels to help you create masks.

Combining Channels

You combine channels when you want to recombine the separate channels into an RGB image. After splitting an image into its separate channels to do some work on it via the channels, such as repairing blemishes in a photo, you need to recombine the channels into a full-color image.

Combining channels into an image requires a little more work but is still relatively easy.

To combine channels into an image, choose Color, Channel Combining and then choose Combine from RGB, HSL, or CMYK, depending on what the image was split into.

Paint Shop Pro displays a dialog box that will enable you to enter the filenames of the channels. Normally, these files would already be open and onscreen from a previous channel splitting.

Identifying the Information in Channels

Now that you've seen how to split an image into its component channels and know how to recombine the channels, it's time to see what channels look like.

Figure 13.1 shows an image with a medium grey background with the words Red, Green, and Blue on it.

FIGURE 13.1.

Red, green, and blue text on a grey background.

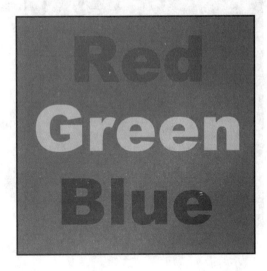

13

Each word is in its own color. That is, the word *Red* is colored red (R: 255, G: 0, B: 0); the word *Green* is in green (R: 0, G: 255, B: 0); and the word *Blue* is in blue (R: 0, G: 0, B: 255). Figures 13.2 through 13.4 show the Red, Green, and Blue channels of Figure 13.1.

FIGURE 13.2.

The Red channel of Figure 13.1.

FIGURE 13.3.

The Green channel of Figure 13.1.

Figure 13.4.

The Blue channel of Figure 13.1.

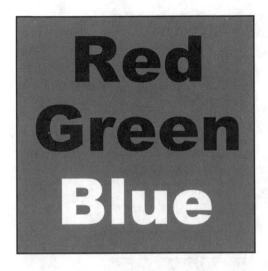

Each channel shows its associated word (color) in white and the other words in black because each color shows up this way in its own channel. If I had left the background of the image white before splitting it into the separate RGB channels, the words in the color of each channel would not be visible.

In other words, a color shows up very brightly in its own channel. The example I used has each color in its purest form, but the theory holds true for any image.

For example, the skin of a Caucasian is made up of mostly red and green with almost no blue at all. Given that, how would you expect the three RGB channels of a portrait to look? If you expect that the skin would be lighter in the Red and Green channels and darker in the Blue channel, you would be right.

Putting Channels to Work

Take a look at the photo of Zoë again (see Figure 13.5).

Of course, you can't see the colors here, but you know what Caucasian skin tones look like. Figures 13.6 through 13.8 are, respectively, the Red, Green, and Blue channels from this photo.

13

FIGURE 13.5.

Color photo of Zoë.

FIGURE 13.6.

Red channel from color photo of Zoë.

FIGURE 13.7.

Green channel from color photo of Zoë.

FIGURE 13.8.

Blue channel from color photo of Zoë.

Notice how the Red and Green channels are quite light and the Blue channel is very dark around Zoë's face? This effect confirms what I said about Caucasian skin being mostly red and green. (Remember that the brighter the areas in the photograph, the more that color appears there. When viewing the Red and Green channels, Zoë's face is very bright. Therefore, in the original image her face contains a lot of red and green. However, when viewing the Blue channel, Zoë's face appears very dark, which shows that her face contains very little blue.)

Testing Your Understanding of Channels

Here's a little exercise to test your knowledge of channels so far. Take a look at the three channels and see whether you can guess the color of Zoë's pajamas. You may not get the exact color, but you should get close.

The pajamas contain a lot of red, as evidenced by how light that portion of the photo is in the Red channel. There's also just a little blue and almost no green.

If you said pale red, pink, or a light pinkish mauve, you'd be right on the money.

13

Using Channels to Create Masks

So how do channels help you, the digital artist? You now know that channels are greyscale representations of the components of an image. You also know what a channel looks like in relation to other channels, and you know a little about reading a channel's information. But what can you do with a channel?

One really good use is to help you make selections and masks that are otherwise some-what difficult to create. Finding the channel with the greatest contrast between the area you want to mask and the rest of the image enables you to create better masks with less work.

Remember how much work was involved in creating the mask around the subject in Hour 12, "Masks"? Take another look at Figures 13.6 through 13.8.

Can you spot a channel that would make the mask creation easier? What about Figure 13.6? A lot of contrast appears along the edges between Zoë and the blanket. It might be easier to work on that channel.

Because splitting an image into its component channels doesn't affect the actual image, you can split the image into its channels and work on one of the channels without harming the original.

For example, I could take the Red channel from the photo of Zoë and further manipulate it to prepare it for building the mask. Figure 13.9 is the result of adjusting the brightness and contrast of the Red channel.

FIGURE 13.9.

Red channel from color photo of Zoë with the brightness and contrast adjusted.

I've added to the brightness and the contrast to boost the difference between Zoë and her blanket. This is still not as good as it could be, though. Instead of trying this channel, I'd rather look for a better way. I'll try splitting the image into the HSL channels.

To see the HSL channels of an image, choose Colors, Channel Splitting, Split to HSL.

The Saturation channel with the differences between Zoë and her blanket is even better than the Red channel was. I'll go with the Saturation channel for the mask creation.

Figure 13.10 shows the Saturation channel from the photo of Zoë.

FIGURE 13.10.

Saturation channel from color photo of Zoë.

By adjusting the brightness and contrast of this channel, you can almost create the mask just by making a selection with the Magic Wand tool.

Figure 13.11 is the result of adjusting the contrast to its highest setting and playing with the brightness a little.

FIGURE 13.11.

Saturation channel from color photo of Zoë with the brightness and contrast adjusted.

13

Notice the black area surrounding Zoë? You could just select this area with the Magic Wand tool, convert the selection to a mask (Masks, New, Hide Selection), and clean up the mask a little with the Paint Brushes tool.

This approach would be easier and result in a better mask than the steps used in Hour 12. Figure 13.12 shows the result of the preceding process.

FIGURE 13.12.

Saturation channel adjusted and turned into a mask.

Aside from some cleanup in the lower-left corner, this mask is almost ready to go. Most of the edges have been selected without my having to paint along them with the Paint Brushes tool.

Summary

In this hour, you learned how to read the information stored in channels, how to split an image into channels, and how to combine channels into an image. You also saw how channels can help you create complex masks.

With some of the seriousness of the last couple of chapters out of the way, I think you'd agree that it's time for a little fun. In the next hour, I discuss picture tubes and show you how they work and how you can create your own.

Workshop

The workshop contains a question and answer section to help answer the most commonly asked questions and quiz questions to help you solidify your understanding of the material covered.

Q&A

Q Why are channels greyscale?

A Channels are greyscale because they represent only one portion of an image—for example, the Red channel (from an RGB split) or the Lightness channel (from an HSL split). The information in any one channel can be described with eight bits. Eight-bit greyscale images are perfectly suited for holding the information that makes up an image's channel.

Q Why would I choose RGB channels over HSL channels?

A The type of channels you split an image into depends on what you hope to accomplish with the channels. As an example, I first looked at RGB channels to create the mask in the last example. However, I ultimately decided to use HSL channels because the Saturation channel came closest to the mask I was trying to create.

Q Does splitting an image into channels affect my original image?

A No. Splitting an image into channels creates completely new images—one for each channel. Even recombining these images (or channels) into an image doesn't affect the original.

Quiz

1. Why would you want to split an image into CMYK channels?
2. Name a good reason for splitting an image into its separate channels.
3. How are channels helpful in creating masks?
4. Do you necessarily need to recombine the channels into an image?

Answers

1. Splitting an image into CMYK channels is necessary for creating color separations for high-end printing.
2. Splitting an image into channels helps you create complex masks more easily than using other methods, such as the ones outlined in Hour 12, for this procedure.
3. By finding the channel with the greatest contrast between the area you want to mask and the rest of the image, you can create better masks with less work.
4. Not if you need the channels for purposes such as creating masks.

13

HOUR 14

Picture Tubes

This hour introduces you to the following issues about picture tubes:

- Understanding picture tubes
- Using picture tubes
- Finding picture tubes
- Creating your own picture tubes

Picture tubes are a new, fun-to-use addition to Paint Shop Pro. They are so much fun, in fact, that many new web sites have sprung up just to offer picture tubes to Paint Shop Pro users. You learn about where you can get more picture tubes later in the hour.

Let's get started by learning what picture tubes are and how they can help you.

What Are Picture Tubes?

Picture tubes, in their most basic form, are really just a form of the Paint Brushes tool. The Picture Tube tool is almost like a rubber stamp in that it allows you to reproduce the same image, or set of images, again and again across a background. The images within a picture tube are set and cannot be modified, but can be reproduced with ease. You can use this technique to create seamless backgrounds, backgrounds for logos, or anything else that follows a theme.

You use the Picture Tube tool much as you do any of the other painting and drawing tools—by selecting it and clicking-and-dragging the mouse. Figure 14.1 shows the Picture Tube tool icon.

Using Picture Tubes

The Picture Tube tool is available in the Tool palette. It's the sixth icon from the bottom (or right, depending on how you have your Toolbar positioned) and looks like a brush with a small blue rubber stamp above it.

After selecting the Picture Tube tool, you can choose the actual tube and the scaling for the image that the tool creates from within the Controls palette (see Figure 14.1).

FIGURE **14.1.**

An image created with the Picture Tube tool and the Controls palette. The Picture Tube tool icon is shown on the right.

To create the image you see in Figure 14.1, follow these steps:

1. Choose the Black Ink Feet tube selection from the Tube menu under the Tool Controls tab in the Controls palette and set the scaling to 100% in the Scale slider.
2. Simply click a few times within the image to draw the feet using the tool.

At this point, if you click the Brush Tip tab in the Controls palette, the options are greyed out. You cannot set them because the only control you have over the picture tube is the actual tube and its scaling. You can't control the color of the images that the Picture Tube tool paints by changing the foreground or background colors, either.

All the information that a tube needs is stored within the tube itself. The good news here is that you can create amazingly complex tubes.

Figure 14.2, for example, is a picture of a tarantula created with one single stroke of the Picture Tube tool.

FIGURE 14.2.

A complex image created with a single stroke of the Picture Tube tool.

Some of the other options available when you're painting with tubes are accessible by clicking on the Options button in the Controls palette after you've selecting the Picture Tube tool (see Figure 14.3).

FIGURE 14.3.

The Picture Tube Options dialog box.

14

From within the Picture Tube Options dialog box, you can set the following settings:

- The Placement mode determines whether the objects in the tube image appear at random or at fixed intervals as you're painting with the Picture Tube tool.
- The Selection mode determines how an object is selected from among the other objects that make up the tube. The Selection modes you can choose from are Random (an object is chosen randomly from among all of the objects); Incremental (objects are chosen in the order in which they are laid out in the tube); Angular (objects are chosen based on the angle at which you click-and-drag the tool); Pressure (objects are chosen based on the amount of pressure you apply with a pen and tablet); and Velocity (objects are chosen based on how fast you move the mouse pointer over the image you are painting on).

Take a moment to try out the various tubes. Play with the scaling, change the tubes, and paint a few strokes with each. You may be amazed at the cool artwork that can be created by combining some of the different tubes.

Finding New Picture Tubes

Even with the substantial number of tubes available when you install Paint Shop Pro, you'll probably find yourself wanting more.

> You can find tons of tubes on the web. As a starting point, visit Jasc Software Inc.'s site at http://www.jasc.com and go to the resources pages. You'll find plenty of sites listed there that offer free tubes.

Tubes are stored as separate files with the Paint Shop Pro folders on the hard drive of any Paint Shop Pro user. This means that users can trade tubes with ease.

You can find the tube files in the Tube folder on your hard drive. To do so, if you installed Paint Shop Pro in its default directory, double-click the My Computer icon on the main Windows desktop. Double-click the C: drive icon, the Program Files icon, the Paint Shop Pro icon, and, finally, the Tubes icon (this order depends on your having installed Paint Shop Pro to the default directory).

After all the double-clicking, you'll see the Tubes folder (see Figure 14.4).

FIGURE 14.4.

The Tubes folder on the author's hard drive.

The icons with the .tub extension are tube files. You can copy any of these, or any you create, to a floppy or add them to an email attachment to send to a friend.

Note that the .tub files you see in this folder are available to you under the Controls palette when the Picture Tube tool is selected.

> If you are having trouble finding the Picture Tube files on your (or someone else's) hard drive, use the Find Files option in the Start menu and search for *.tub. This search finds any files on the current hard drive with the .tub extension.

As well, you can zip them up singly or in groups and store them on a web site so that anyone in the world can access them. Before you do so, though, you have to create some of your own tubes.

Creating Your Own Picture Tubes

Creating your own picture tubes is, naturally, more complicated than just painting with them. It's not all that difficult, though.

There are just a few things to keep in mind. You must create your tubes on a transparent background, and it must be 24-bit color. As well, you must break up the main tube image (the image that will hold the various tubes or objects) into a grid and place each separate image into one of the squares formed by the grid.

14

You'll need to set up the grid so that it has enough squares to hold your images. You can use as few as one square and as many squares as you'll need to accommodate the various objects you'll be using. I'm not sure what the limit on squares is, but without going through each built-in tube, I came across some that went as high as 36 squares.

The first step is to decide which objects to use. Normally, you want a theme of some sort. For the following exercise, I use a few letters, but you can draw images, scan images or objects, copy portions of photographs, or use anything else you'd like.

After you decide on the subject and gather up the objects you need, it's time to build the tube image. Follow these steps:

1. Open a new image that'll be large enough to hold all of the objects you'll be using. Start with a 600×200 image.

2. Remember to set the Background Color to transparent. If you don't, you won't be able to export your image to a tube file—and you'll only find this out after putting all the time and effort into creating and arranging your objects.

   You also won't be able to export the image to a tube file if you have more than one layer in the image. If you keep these things in mind before starting out, you'll be okay.

3. With your new image file open, you can turn on the grid to help you with the placement of your various objects. To turn on the grid, choose View, Grid.

4. Of course, the grid may not be set up with the dimensions you need. To correct this problem, choose File, Preferences, General Program Preferences. You will get the Paint Shop Pro Preferences dialog box.

5. Click the Rulers and Units tab to display these options (see Figure 14.5).

FIGURE 14.5.

The Rulers and Units tab.

6. You'll need to set the Horizontal and Vertical Spacing settings to the size you need for your grid. Because I'll be creating three objects in a 600×200 image, I set the spacing to 200. This setting gives me three 200×200 squares across.

7. I also set the Line Color to a bright red. I did so because the default, grey, which works nicely on a white background without getting in the way, isn't too visible on the transparent background. To change the color of the grid's lines, click the Change button and select a color from the Color Picker dialog box.

8. Finally, click OK to set the new grid preferences.

Figure 14.6 shows my image with the grid turned on and set up with the dimensions and color I selected.

FIGURE 14.6.

Empty image file with the grid visible.

After you open the new image and set up the grid, you can start placing or drawing your objects.

1. I chose to use the letters *A, B,* and *C.* To place these letters (or any image) into the grid, you simply move the object into place while it's still selected.

2. After placing the letters into the grid, I decided to jazz them up a bit.

   I used the Blade Pro plug-in on the letter *A* (I show you more about this and other plug-ins in Hour 15, "Applying Filters"), played around with some noise and some motion blurring to get the metallic effect for the letter *B,* and used the woodgrain texture effect from Hour 10, "Creating Cool Text Effects," to create the letter *C.*

The final image appears in Figure 14.7.

FIGURE 14.7.

ABC image file ready to be exported to a tube file.

14

All that's left is to export the image as a tube file, as follows:

1. Make sure that the image you want to export is open and that it's the current image. Then choose File, Export, Picture Tube to open the Export Picture Tube dialog box (see Figure 14.8).

FIGURE **14.8.**

The Export Picture Tube dialog box.

2. The only settings you'll need to change are the numbers for Cells Across and Cells Down. Change these to reflect the number of cells that your image contains. For this example, I would choose three cells across and one cell down. The total number of cells will be updated automatically for you. You can pretty much ignore the other options; the tube's user can set them. However, you do need to give your tube a name.

After you make the changes and enter a name, you can click OK in the Export Picture Tube dialog box to save your tube.

Your tube will be available immediately. To test it, open a new file (you can change the background from transparent to any color you choose at this point), select the Picture Tube tool, choose your tube from the pull-down menu in the Controls palette, and start painting.

That's it!

You should have lots of fun with tubes. Remember that you can change the size of the squares when you create a tube image; you don't need to use the 200×200 that I did. You can use from 1 to 36 (at least, maybe more) squares, and you can fill the squares with just about anything you want.

Try rotating your objects or resizing them (see Hour 6, "Working with Deformations," for a refresher on using deformations) as you place them in the grid. Try using similar objects but with different colors, and so on.

Summary

I hope you enjoyed this hour as much as I did. I think tubes are fun, and you should have some fun using and creating them. In this hour, you learned how to use existing tubes, how to find new tubes, how to create your own tubes, and how to share the tubes you create with others.

The topic of filters, both built-in and third party, is one of my favorites, and you'll see why in the next hour.

Workshop

The workshop contains a question and answer section to help answer the most commonly asked questions and quiz questions to help you solidify your understanding of the material covered.

Q&A

Q I get an error when I try to export my tube image; why?

A You must make sure that the image is 24-bit color, that it contains only one layer, and that the objects are placed over a transparency. Improperly setting these options is the most common reason for such an error message.

Q Can I use pictures of people for tubes?

A Yes. Anything that can be scanned in or drawn can be used. All you need to do is copy the portions of the images you want and paste them into the image that you'll be exporting as a tube.

Q When I try drawing with some tubes, only one object shows up. Why?

A Check to see whether the tube contains more than one image and what the Selection mode is. You can check these settings by clicking the Options button in the Controls palette with the Picture Tube tool selected. If the Pressure setting is set for the Selection mode and you're using a mouse instead of a tablet, you might only get one of the objects from the tube to show up.

Quiz

1. How do you view the grid to help you place objects when creating a tube file?
2. How do you change the dimensions and color of the grid lines?

14

3. How many grids can you use when creating a tube file?

4. How can you share your tube files with others?

Answers

1. Choose View, Grid.

2. Choose File, Preferences, General Program Preferences. The grid settings can be changed in the Paint Shop Pro Preferences dialog box under the Rulers and Units tab.

3. You can create from 1 to 36 (and possibly more) grids. You just need to create the grid and store your objects in it. When you export the file, enter the appropriate numbers in the Cells Across and Cells Down fields.

4. Tube files are stored on your hard drive in a folder under the Paint Shop Pro folder. Any of the .tub files can be copied to floppy, attached to email messages, or placed on a web site where others can access them.

Hour **15**

Applying Filters

Filters, a type of built-in or third-party plug-in, are extensions to a program. Filters add functionality to a program by allowing you to create an effect that you otherwise could not create. Some filters come with Paint Shop Pro, and other filters (often referred to as plug-ins) are available from third-party software companies.

In this hour, I show you some of the built-in filters as well as some of my favorite third-party plug-ins. I also show you some of the cool effects that you can accomplish with these filters. The following issues are covered:

- Understanding filters
- Finding cool filters
- Using Paint Shop Pro's built-in filters
- Installing plug-ins
- Using third-party filters

Why Filters?

As I mentioned, filters, or plug-ins, extend the capabilities of a program such as Paint Shop Pro.

Many of today's imaging programs are written to be *extensible*, which means that they can have their functionality extended through the use of add-on software. This technology enables other programmers to write software that can literally be plugged-in to the main program.

If you've purchased and installed a plug-in program, it should be available under the Image, Plug-in Filters menu in Paint Shop Pro.

Where You Can Get Filters

As I said, some filters come with Paint Shop Pro and others are available from third parties. Most, if not all, of the companies that write plug-ins are on the web, and some offer free demos of their plug-ins.

Plug-ins range from free (or nearly free) to shareware (priced from $15 to $25) to commercial products (priced from $50 to $200 or more).

The web addresses of several companies mentioned in this hour follow.

- Alien Skin at `http://www.alienskin.com`. Alien Skin makes the very popular Eye Candy plug-in.

- Auto F/X at `http://www.autofx.com`. Auto F/X makes plug-ins such as Page Edges, Photo/Graphic Edges, Typo/Graphic Edges, The Ultimate Texture Collection, and more.

- Flaming Pear at `http://www.ccn.cs.dal.ca/~aa731/blade.html`. Flaming Pear is the creator of BladePro, a relatively new, but increasingly popular, plug-in that enables you to add textures and bevels to objects.

- Metacreations at `http://www.metacreations.com`. Metacreations, widely known for its 2D and 3D imaging products, also produces Kai's Power Tools (KPT). KPT is a collection of awesome filters that enable you to create gradients and textures and to manipulate images.

- RAYflect at `http://www.rayflect.com`. RAYflect products include Four Seasons, which enables you to add realistic and otherworldly atmospheric backdrops (skies such as sunsets, storms, and so on) to your images.

- Wacom at `http://www.wacom.com`. If you're lucky enough to own a Wacom graphics tablet, you should also have a copy of PenTools. PenTools, which ships with every tablet from Wacom, offers a collection of cool effects that work with your pen and tablet.

I don't cover all the filters available on the market (there are just too many with more coming to market weekly, it seems). Whole books could be written on the subject. I don't even cover each separate filter in any given package (again, there are just too many). However, I do show you some of my favorites, give you an idea of how to use them, and suggest what you can accomplish with them.

Using Built-in Filters

You've already seen examples of at least one of the built-in filters. I've used the Hot Wax Coating filter a couple of times to add texture and to create a chrome effect. Paint Shop Pro has a few more built-in filters, though, and the nicest are the Effects filters.

The Effects filters consist of Buttonize, Chisel, Cutout, and Drop Shadow. Each is discussed in the following sections.

Buttonize Filter

The Buttonize filter (choose Image, Effects, Buttonize) enables you to instantly create rectangular buttons from any image. Figure 15.1 shows the Buttonize dialog box.

FIGURE 15.1.

A button being created with the Buttonize filter and the Buttonize dialog box.

You can see the settings I've chosen for the button and the results of applying those settings in Figure 15.1.

You can change the height, width, and opacity of the bevel. Also, you can choose from a solid or a transparent edge. You can also use the Auto Proof feature so that you can see the changes you're applying in real time.

Both the Solid Edge and the Transparent Edge options use the current background color for the bevel. The difference is that the solid edge is a solid color, using only shades of the background color, whereas the transparent edge allows the image to show through, as seen in Figure 15.1.

Chisel Filter

The Chisel filter (choose Image, Effects, Chisel) adds an outer bevel around the current selection. This bevel can be transparent or in the background color. You can also adjust the size of the bevel.

You can see the effects of the bevel in the preview window of the dialog box in Figure 15.2.

In this dialog box, you can set the size of the bevel and whether or not it should be transparent or created with the current background color.

Cutout Filter

The Cutout filter (choose Image, Effects, Cutout) makes selections appear to be cut out of the background. Essentially, this filter adds a shadow to the inside of the object (see Figure 15.3).

FIGURE 15.3.

The Cutout effect being applied to some text.

You can choose to have the area filled with white if you like. You can also set the Interior and Shadow colors, the Opacity and Blur of the shadow, and the Vertical and Horizontal offsets of the shadow.

The Vertical and Horizontal offsets enable you to move the shadow around to get different effects.

The Blur setting also affects this feature. A softer blur makes the cutout appear higher than the same effect done with less blurring.

The Opacity setting affects how opaque or transparent the resulting shadow will be.

Drop Shadow Filter

The Drop Shadow effect adds a drop shadow to selected objects. This effect is often used on text.

You can set the Color, the Opacity, and the Blur of the shadow. You can also set the Vertical and Horizontal offsets of the shadow effect (see Figure 15.4).

One effect that I like is to apply the drop shadow to white text on a white background (see Figure 15.5).

FIGURE 15.4.

The Drop Shadow effect being applied to some text.

FIGURE 15.5.

The Drop Shadow effect applied to white text on a white background.

To create this effect, open a new image with a white background and then follow these steps:

1. Set the foreground color to white and select the Text tool.

2. Add some text to your image.

3. Instead of filled text, you'll see just a selection. (The text is still filled; it's just filled with white and is against a white background.)

4. Choose Image, Effects, Drop Shadow and set the options to your liking.

5. After clicking OK to apply the drop shadow, you should end up with a result similar to that shown in Figure 15.5.

   I've seen this effect used recently on television and in magazine ads. Hard to believe that it's so simple.

Recall also that many of the filters discussed in this hour are used throughout various parts of the book. In Hour 10, "Creating Cool Text Effects," for example, I used the

15

Gaussian Blur filter for the *X-Files* text, and in Hour 11, "Layers," I used the Emboss filter to give a relief effect to an object on a woodgrain.

I show you how some of the other built-in filters can be applied throughout this entire book.

Using Third-Party Filters

Along with the filters that ship with Paint Shop Pro, numerous third-party filters (plug-ins) are available.

Installing Plug-Ins

Installing a plug-in package so that it can be used with Paint Shop Pro is a multistep process:

1. The first step is installing the software according to the manufacturer's instructions. These days that mostly involves inserting a CD-ROM into the drive and following a couple of short instructions.

   The most important point to note is where on your hard drive the plug-ins are installed.

   Normally, you'll want to keep all of your plug-ins in separate folders under one main folder. You may, for example, create a Plug-ins folder under the Paint Shop Pro folder and store all your plug-ins in separate folders there.

2. The second step to installing your plug-ins is telling Paint Shop Pro where they are on your hard drive, which is the reason behind making a Plug-ins folder. After you've installed your plug-ins, choose File, Preferences, General Program Preferences.

3. Choose the Plug-in Filters tab to bring up the Plug-in Filters options (see Figure 15.6).

FIGURE 15.6.

*The Plug-in Filters
options.*

4. Enter the folder(s) where the filters are stored into the text box(es) at the bottom of the dialog box. For example, in Figure 15.6, I have entered C:\Program Files\Paint Shop Pro 5\Plugins in the first folder area. You can also click the Browse button to find the appropriate folder instead of typing in the name. I've enabled two entries because I own Paint Shop Pro (in Folder 1) as well as Photoshop (in Folder 2). I keep most of my filters under the Photoshop folder.

The options you can set in the Plug-in Filters tab are as follows:

- Enable Filters—This option allows the use of external image processing filters. You should, of course, place a checkmark next to this option if you want to use the filters you've installed.

- Include Subfolders When Searching for Filters—This option should be checked if you've done as I recommended and stored each plug-in package in its own sub-folder.

- Limit Loaded Plug-in Files to Those with an .8B*x* Extension Only—This option should be checked if all the filters (which is most of those available) are 100% Photoshop compatible. Paint Shop Pro enables you to use external plug-ins that are compatible with the industry standard. That standard is set by Adobe, the maker of Photoshop. Photoshop-compatible filters have a file extension that starts with 8B and ends with one other character. Normally, using only this type of filter results in fewer compatibility problems.

- Enable Plug-in Automatic File Format Identification—You can leave this option unchecked, as I have done, or you can let Paint Shop Pro try to identify the file format of your plug-in filters.

- Folder Names—As mentioned previously, these next three entries in the dialog box are the most important. They tell Paint Shop Pro where to find your plug-ins.

With your plug-ins installed and with Paint Shop Pro made aware of where they are, you should be able to find them under Image, Plug-in Filters.

If you've installed Export filters, such as Ulead's SmartSaver, they will also be available under File, Export, Plug-in Export. Note that if you install filters while Paint Shop Pro is running, you might have to restart the program before the filters are available.

15

Alien Skin's Eye Candy

Eye Candy has long been one of my favorite plug-ins. It has some cool filters such as Inner Bevel, Chrome, Fire, and Smoke. Figure 15.7 shows the Eye Candy dialog box for the Smoke filter.

FIGURE 15.7.

Alien Skin's Eye Candy dialog box for the Smoke filter.

The Eye Candy dialog boxes are pretty much the same for all filters. The only changes are the particular options you can set.

One nice touch with the Eye Candy filters is the real-time preview window, which you can see in the lower-right corner of Figure 15.7. Figure 15.8 shows the result of applying both the Fire and the Smoke filters.

FIGURE 15.8.

Alien Skin's Fire and Smoke filters applied to some text in Paint Shop Pro.

I've seen many tips on applying a fire effect to text, but none comes close to the Eye Candy filter. You can get a demo of the Eye Candy filters at Alien Skin's web site (`http://www.alienskin.com`).

Auto F/X's Photo/Graphic Edges

Auto F/X is the creator of several amazing filter packages. One of my favorites is Photo/Graphic Edges.

Starting with the latest version, Photo/Graphic Edges operates as a standalone as well as a plug-in. That is, you can run it separately as well as from within Paint Shop Pro.

The Photo/Graphic Edges filter enables you to add complex edges to your photographs. Also, you can add certain effects such as Sepia Tones, Grain, and Burn. Figure 15.9 shows the Photo/Graphic Edges dialog box.

FIGURE 15.9.

Auto F/X's Photo/Graphic Edges dialog box.

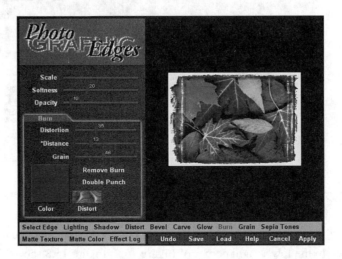

Figure 15.10 is the result of adding both an edge and a burn effect to a photograph of some fall leaves.

Along with the various effects that can be applied to an image with the Photo/Graphic Edges filter, you can select from a large gallery of edges that comes with the plug-in.

Visit Auto F/X's web site at `http://www.autofx.com` for more information and to download a demo of this cool plug-in.

FIGURE 15.10.

Auto F/X's Photo/Graphic Edges filter applied to a photograph of some fall leaves.

Flaming Pear's BladePro

There is a lot of fuss over this "new kid on the block" on the Paint Shop Pro Internet newsgroup (`comp.graphics.apps.paint-shop-pro`), and rightly so. This really cool plug-in enables you to add textures, lighting, and bevels to your images. All you need to do is select an object and call up the filter (Image, Plug-in Filters, Flaming Pear, BladePro).

Figure 15.11 shows a template I created for my web site, GrafX Design (`http://www.grafx-design.com`) a while back.

FIGURE 15.11.

Radioactivity symbol template created in CorelDRAW for the GrafX Design web site.

I used BladePro (see Figure 15.12) to add a prebuilt texture called Lizard to the symbol after selecting it with the Magic Wand tool.

FIGURE 15.12.

Flaming Pear's BladePro dialog box.

The result of applying the texture can be seen in Figure 15.13.

FIGURE 15.13.

The Lizard texture from Flaming Pear's BladePro plug-in applied to the radioactivity symbol.

In addition to the extra textures and environments supplied with BladePro, many more are available from the Flaming Pear web site (`http://www.ccn.cs.dal.ca/~aa731/blade.html`) and from other sites springing up all over the web.

Typing **BladePro** into your favorite Internet search engine will undoubtedly turn up hundreds of sites where you can find more textures and environments for BladePro.

You can, of course, play around with the settings of the various options to create your own effects. These can be saved and passed on to friends or placed on your own web site to be shared with the rest of the world.

To save a setting, click on the bottom button at the middle of the interface. Clicking this button will bring up a dialog box where you can name and save your settings file.

15

RAYflect's Four Seasons

RAYflect's Four Seasons is an atmospheric generator. Huh? Okay, let's try this again. The Four Seasons plug-in enables you to create sky scenes such as sunsets, sunrises, and even rainbows. In fact, the rainbow effect in Figure 15.1 at the beginning of this hour's discussion was created with the Four Seasons plug-in.

You can use this filter to fill in those terribly plain or washed-out, pale blue skies that you sometimes get in photographs. For example, the train in Figure 15.14 was shot on a cloudy, rainy day in New Hampshire.

FIGURE 15.14.

Shot of an old railway engine.

Although the grey day did wonders for bringing out the saturated colors of the engine, the sky itself really detracts from the overall feel of the photograph. No problem—Four Seasons to the rescue.

Using the selection and masking techniques described in Hour 3, "Opening, Saving, and Printing Files," and Hour 12, "Masks," I selected the sky and was then able to run the RAYflect plug-in (see Figure 15.15) to give the sky a major facelift.

FIGURE 15.15.

*RAYflect's Four
Seasons dialog box.*

You can use the Four Seasons plug-in to adjust the sun, the moon, and the clouds. You
can add haze and fog or use one of the preset skies. I used one of the daytime presets to
enhance the sky behind the engine (see Figure 15.16).

FIGURE 15.16.

*Shot of an old railway
engine with an
enhanced sky courtesy
of RAYflect's Four
Seasons plug-in.*

Visit RAYflect's web site at `http://www.rayflect.com` to download a demo of this
plug-in when you want to add a bit of color to the skies in a photograph.

Other Plug-Ins

You can start finding cool plug-ins by checking out the demos of the ones I've mentioned here and the others listed at the beginning of this hour. You're sure to find a product that meets your needs, whether it's to enhance your photographs or to help in the creation of web graphics.

15

Summary

I hope you enjoyed this hour. It was more of a reading and visual adventure than a hands-on experience. I wanted to use this time to give you an idea of what's available out there in the way of plug-ins, though, rather than just walk you through one or two examples.

I hope that you got an idea of why the topic of filters, both built-in and third party, is one of my favorites. Filters really are fun to play with and, more than that, they can really add to your images in many ways.

Workshop

The workshop contains a question and answer section to help answer the most commonly asked questions and quiz questions to help you solidify your understanding of the material covered.

Q&A

Q I tried to apply a filter but the option was greyed out. Why?

A Most filters need you to be running in 16.7 million-color mode and won't work otherwise. Choose Colors, Increase Color Depth, 16.7 Million Colors. If this method doesn't work, make sure that you're trying to apply the filter to an object or selection on the current layer and that the object or selection contains the needed information (make sure that the selection is not empty or transparent).

Q I don't understand the difference between filters and plug-ins. What is the difference?

A Filters are the built-in effects that come with Paint Shop Pro, and plug-ins are usually add-ons. These terms are often interchanged, though.

Q I installed a filter but it doesn't show up in the menu. Why isn't it there?

A The most likely cause is that you haven't told Paint Shop Pro where the filter is stored on your hard drive. Choose File, Preferences, General Program Preferences and click the Plug-in Filters tab. Enter the folder where you installed the plug-in filter into one of the three folder entries in the dialog box. After doing so, your filter should show up. If it doesn't, chances are that you installed the filter while Paint Shop Pro was running. Exit and restart Paint Shop Pro to see whether this step solves the problem.

Quiz

1. Where can you get plug-ins for Paint Shop Pro?
2. How do you install a plug-in?
3. What do plug-ins do?
4. Why would you want to use a filter or plug-in?

Answers

1. Plug-ins are available from many different companies. Many of these companies have web sites. See the list at the beginning of this hour for a starting point.
2. First, install the software according to the manufacturer's instructions. Then open Paint Shop Pro and choose File, Preferences, General Program Preferences. Click the Plug-in Filters tab and enter the folder where the filters are stored into one of the text boxes at the bottom of the dialog box.
3. Essentially, plug-ins extend the functionality of Paint Shop Pro. They do so by enabling you to apply new effects, depending on the plug-in.
4. Plug-ins and filters enable you to create certain effects that would be hard to accomplish, if not impossible, without their use.

PART IV

Advanced Paint Shop Pro Tasks

Hour

HOUR **16**

Special Effects

You should pretty much be at the point now where you can start to take advantage of what you've learned so far. You can start applying your knowledge to create some effects that produce more advanced images.

In this hour, I show you how to create a page curl effect, how to mimic gold and other metallic effects, and how to add bevels to give your images a more 3D look. The following issues are covered:

- Adding a page curl effect
- Creating metallic effects
- Using bevels effectively

Adding a Page Curl Effect

I originally wrote this tutorial for GrafX Design, my web graphics tutorial web site, using CorelDRAW. I then wondered whether I could accomplish the same effect with a bitmap paint program such as Photoshop or Paint Shop Pro.

I discovered that it could be done and subsequently wrote the tutorial for both Photoshop and Paint Shop Pro. They have been very popular tutorials.

This effect, like many others, is actually easier to accomplish with version 5 than it was with previous versions. First, you have to create a Bézier curve. Follow these steps:

1. Open a new image in the size that you want the final image to be. If you're going to use it for a web graphic, I suggest keeping it around 200×250.

2. Set the resolution to 72 pixels per inch, the background color to white, and the image type to 16.7 million colors.

3. Add a new layer by clicking on the Add New Layer icon at the bottom of the Layers palette.

4. Set the foreground color to a bright yellow and use the Flood Fill tool to fill the new layer with yellow.

5. Select the Freehand tool (it's the selection tool that looks like a small lasso).

6. In the Controls palette, set the selection type to point-to-point, set the feather value to 0, and make sure that the anti-alias option is checked.

7. Place the mouse pointer in the lower-left corner of the image (you can use the information in the lower-left corner of the screen to guide you).

8. Click once and place the mouse pointer against the right-hand side of your image and about one-fifth of the way up from the bottom. Click the mouse again.

9. Place the mouse in the lower-right corner of the image and double-click so that it makes a triangular selection.

    You should have a selection similar to that shown in Figure 16.1.

10. Press the Delete key to remove the selected area (see Figure 16.2).

11. Choose Selections, Select None.

12. Click on the yellow foreground color swatch to bring up the Color dialog box.

13. Set the foreground color to a darker shade of yellow. My original yellow was R: 255, G: 255, and B: 0; my darker shade is R: 200, G: 200, and B: 0.

14. Select the Line tool (it's the icon with the diagonal line across it) and, in the Controls palette, set the line type to Bézier, the width to 1, and place a checkmark in the Antialias checkbox.

FIGURE 16.1.

Yellow rectangle with a triangular selection made at the bottom.

16

FIGURE 16.2.

Yellow rectangle with a triangular piece cut from the bottom.

15. Click-and-drag from the lower-right corner of the yellow area up and out a bit until you have a line like the one in Figure 16.3.

FIGURE 16.3.

The first steps in creating a Bézier curve for the page curl effect.

16. Click-and-drag from about the middle of the line and to its left until you get a nice curve like that shown in Figure 16.4; then click a final time.

FIGURE 16.4.

The final Bézier curve created for the page curl effect.

17. Change the line style to normal and draw a line from the upper-left point on the curve to the bottom-left corner of the image (see Figure 16.5).

FIGURE 16.5.

A straight line added to the final Bézier curve.

18. Select the Magic Wand tool (it's the icon that resembles a magician's black-and-white wand with a yellow aura near the top).

19. Click within the area that you've created with the two lines. This step should select the bottom area created by the two lines that you've drawn.

20. Select the Flood Fill tool and click within the selected area to fill it with the current foreground color (which should still be the dark yellow color).

21. Set the foreground color back to the bright yellow. (You can do so quickly by selecting the Dropper tool and clicking anywhere on the image that contains the bright yellow color.)

22. Draw four lines from the lower-left corner of the image out towards the curved line (see Figure 16.6).

FIGURE 16.6.

Four more straight lines added to the curl area.

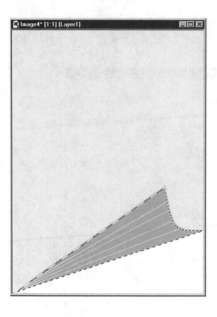

These lines enable you to fill in some of the areas created by the Bézier curve and the first straight line. You will be able to fill in the areas, and they will have the proper perspective as well.

23. Before you start the next steps, save the current selection. Do so by choosing Selections, Save to Alpha Channel. For now, just leave the defaults and click OK on the dialog boxes that show up.

24. Choose Selections, Select None.

25. Choose the Magic Wand tool and, in the Controls palette, set the Match mode to RGB and the Tolerance to 0.

26. Click in the second area (from the top) created by the new yellow lines. Only the second area should be selected. If more of the image is selected, your lines are probably off a bit. Use Edit, Undo a couple of times to get back to where you started the lines and make sure that they are drawn from the lower-left corner of the image up to where the selected area ends at the curve.

27. Choose the Flood Fill tool and fill the area with bright yellow.

28. Select the third, or middle, area with the Magic Wand tool and fill it with white.

29. Select the fourth area created by the lines and fill it with bright yellow.

You image should resemble the one shown in Figure 16.7.

FIGURE 16.7.

Areas created by the four straight lines filled with yellow and white.

16

It's time to reload the saved selection so that you can apply the final steps:

1. Choose Selections, Load from Alpha Channel and choose the selection from the dialog box (it should be the only one there).

2. With the selection loaded, choose Image, Blur, Gaussian Blur and set the value for the radius to about 5.00. Use the Text tool to add some text, such as E.T. Phone Home.

Your final image should resemble the one shown in Figure 16.8.

In the final image (Figure 16.8), I've added a bit of fun text just to show you how the image would look if you were going to use it on a web page, for example. You can use this effect with any color and do it with any corner of the image.

FIGURE 16.8.

*Final page curl effect
with the lower-right
corner curled up.*

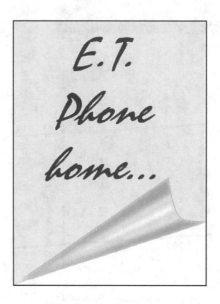

Mastering Metallic Effects

Since I first started GrafX Design, I've received a lot of email asking how to create a
metallic effect. Here's one way that's quick and easy:

1. Open a new 600×600-pixel image with the resolution set to 72 pixels per inch, the
   background color set to white, and the image type set to 16.7 million colors.

2. Choose Image, Noise, Add.

3. In the Add Noise dialog box, set the %Noise to 100 and choose Random. Click
   OK. These settings will fill the image with thousands of small colored pixels.

4. To create the metallic effect, though, you'll want the noise to be greyscale. To
   change the image from color to greyscale, choose Colors, Grey Scale. You're noise
   will now be in shades of grey.

5. It's time to make the noise look like brushed metal. Before you do so, though, you
   should return the color depth to 16.7 million colors. To do so, choose Colors,
   Increase Color Depth, 16.7 Million Colors.

6. Choose Image, Blur, Motion Blur.

7. In the Motion Blur dialog box, set the direction to about 120 degrees and the intensity to about 25 pixels.

You should end up with something like Figure 16.9.

FIGURE 16.9.

The beginnings of a metallic effect.

16

I think that the effect needs a little adjustment before it's ready. Try this:

1. Choose Colors, Adjust, Brightness/Contrast.
2. Lower the brightness to about –6 and bump the contrast up to about 29.

Your final image should resemble brushed aluminum (see Figure 16.10). Save this image or keep it onscreen, as you can use it in the next exercise as well.

You may not be able to see the difference between Figures 16.9 and 16.10 on the printed pages of this book, because of limitations in how images are printed. You will notice a subtle difference on your computer screen if you create the image yourself by following the steps I've used.

This texture can be used for all types of features from interfaces to text.

Figure 16.10.

Final brushed aluminum effect.

Using Bevels

It used to be that you'd need to resort to third-party plug-ins if you wanted a good inner bevel effect for interfaces, oddly shaped buttons, and text. With version 5's capabilities, though, you can now add bevels to any shape you desire. Here's how:

1. Open a new 600×300-pixel image with the resolution set to 72 pixels per inch, the background color set to white, and the image type set to 16.7 million colors.

2. Set the foreground color to black and, using the Text tool, add some text to the image. I used Arial Black at 100 points with the style set to Bold Italic (see Figure 16.11).

Figure 16.11.

Black, bold, italic, Arial text on a white background.

3. With the text still selected (it should be selected right after you add it to the image), save the selection to an alpha channel by choosing Selections, Save to Alpha Channel. Leave the defaults for now.

4. Choose Selections, Select None to deselect the text.

5. Choose Image, Blur, Gaussian Blur and use a value of 2.00 for the radius.

6. Choose Image, Other, Emboss. You should now have some nicely embossed text (see Figure 16.12).

16

FIGURE 16.12.

Bevel effect added to the text with the Emboss filter.

It's kind of dull in grey, though. This problem can definitely be fixed.

7. Choose Selections, Load from Alpha Channel. This step brings back the original selection, and it will surround the beveled text. It's a little too small, though.

8. To fix that, choose Selections, Modify, Expand, and enter a value of 2.

9. To get rid of the background, set the background color to white and choose Selections, Invert. Press Delete to fill the area around the text with white.

10. Choose Selections, Invert once more to select the text.

11. If you still have that metallic texture that you created in the last exercise handy, make it current by clicking its title bar. If you saved it, simply reload it.

12. Choose Selections, Select All.

13. Choose Edit, Copy. Make the text image current.

14. Add a new layer by clicking the Add New Layer icon at the bottom of the Layers palette. The selection that surrounds the text should still be active.

15. Choose Edit, Paste, Into Selection. Doing so fills the selection with the metallic effect.

16. Change the layer's blending mode to Overlay. You should be able to see the bevel effect through the metallic texture.

17. The metallic texture is a little light, though. Choose Colors, Adjust, Brightness/Contrast.

18. Set the brightness to –29 and the contrast to 29 to darken the metallic effect.

Your final image should resemble Figure 16.13.

FIGURE 16.13.

Beveled metallic text.

You can fill the text with any texture you want. You may have to change the numbers used for the brightness and contrast, though.

Figure 16.14 was created with the same steps as the image in Figure 16.13 except that I filled the text in Figure 16.14 with a texture from Kai's Power Tools.

FIGURE 16.14.

Beveled textured text.

Summary

I hope you enjoyed this hour. Paint Shop Pro also enables you to create many other special effects. Examples appear throughout this book; many more are in my other Paint Shop Pro book, *Paint Shop Pro Web Techniques*, New Riders Publishing, ISBN: 1-56205-756-1 (even though that book was written with Paint Shop Pro 4, a lot of the techniques still apply); and tons more are on the web. You can start with some of the effects on my GrafX Design web site (`http://www.grafx-design.com`), find others at Jasc Software, Inc.'s, web site, and still others at links from Jasc and GrafX Design.

As you become more familiar with Paint Shop Pro and with digital imaging in general, you'll probably come up with many more effects yourself.

Workshop

The workshop contains a question and answer section to help answer the most commonly asked questions and quiz questions to help you solidify your understanding of the material covered.

Q&A

Q Where can I find more effects that can be created with Paint Shop Pro?

A A good starting place is the web. You can visit Jasc Software's site at http://www.jasc.com and GrafX Design at http://www.grafx-design.com. Both sites contain tips and links to other sites with even more tips.

Q Can I make different colored metals like gold and bronze?

A Yes. One way is to experiment with colorizing the image. Choose Colors, Colorize and play around with the Hue and the Saturation settings.

Q Is there an easier way to do page curls?

A Yes. A third-party filter is available in Kai's Power Tools from Metacreations.

Quiz

1. How do you save the current selection to an alpha channel, and why would you want to do so?

2. What is a bevel?

3. What is a Bézier curve, and how do you create one?

4. How does the Magic Wand tool help you build special effects?

Answers

1. You save the current selection to an alpha channel by choosing Selections, Save to Alpha Channel. Saving to an alpha channel saves the selection you've made along with the image.

2. A bevel is, in real life anyway, an angled area around the edges of an object. This effect can be "faked" in a paint program, such as Paint Shop Pro, to add apparent depth to an image.

16

3. A Bézier curve is drawn on a computer screen, using a mathematical formula invented by the French mathematician Bézier. Bézier's formula allows for very smooth curves.

4. You can use the Magic Wand tool to select portions of various objects based on their colors.

HOUR 17

Retouching Your Images

We all have a collection of snapshots that we cherish, right? Or we have a collection of old family photos, a few of which we'd like to frame and put up on a wall. Some of these images are in good shape but, more often than not, some of them need at least some retouching.

Paint Shop Pro has the tools you need to fix all but the worst of your images. This hour covers the following issues:

- Using the retouching tools
- Fixing brightness and contrast
- Removing dust marks and scratches
- Removing portions of an image

Using the Retouching Tools

Several problems usually need correcting. Old snapshots often have scratches, dust spots, and bad brightness and contrast; sometimes they have a less-than-sharp image because of the quality of the older camera lens.

You can fix the dust spots and scratches by using a combination of the Dropper, the Paint Brushes, the Retouch, and the Clone Brush tools. In addition, you can fix most brightness and contrast problems by using the Brightness/Contrast feature, and you can fix the sharpness by using the Unsharp Mask filter.

I show you how to use each of these tools as I walk you through the process of fixing the image you see in Figure 17.1.

FIGURE 17.1.

Old family photograph in need of repair.

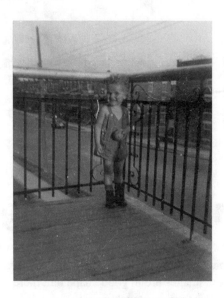

You can see that all the problems mentioned earlier exist in this particular photo. There are dust spots and a couple of scratches, the brightness and contrast are off, and the photo is not as sharp as it could be. I'll fix each of these problems in this hour, starting with the brightness and contrast.

Fixing the Brightness and Contrast

To adjust the brightness and contrast of an image choose Colors, Adjust, Brightness/Contrast.

Using the preview window, I bumped up the contrast of this image to +12 and left the brightness alone. You can see the results, along with the Brightness/Contrast dialog box, in Figure 17.2.

Figure 17.2.

*Adjusting the bright-
ness and contrast.*

17

You can see the original image to the left in the dialog box, and you can see the effect of the changes in the preview window to the right. You can click-and-drag the preview window, as well, so that you can see different areas of the image.

You can also zoom in and out on the preview by selecting the Zoom tool (it's the one that resembles a magnifying glass) and left-clicking to zoom in and right-clicking to zoom out.

If zooming doesn't show you as much of the image as you'd like, you can place a checkmark in the Auto Proof checkbox, as I've done, so that the changes will be visible in the image itself.

With the brightness and contrast adjusted, the next step is to remove the dust spots and scratches.

Removing Dust Marks and Scratches

You'll want to remove as many of the dust marks and scratches as you can before using the Unsharp Mask filter because this filter can actually accentuate the bad spots of a photograph.

Removing the spots is tedious but fairly easy. I recommend a combination of the Dropper and the Paint Brushes tools. (This process involves switching between the two tools, picking up nearby colors with the Dropper, and applying them with the Paint Brushes tool.) Follow these steps:

1. Zoom in on the image so that you can easily spot the dust marks you'll need to fix.

2. Select the Dropper (its icon resembles a small eyedropper) and use it to select a color near a spot that needs to be repaired. Switch to the Paint Brushes tool to paint over the dust mark. (Make sure first that the brush is set to a small size and that the hardness is low [even setting it to 0] and that the opacity is about 50%.)

   You'll need to be constantly switching between the Dropper to pick up a new color and the Paint Brushes tool to paint over a dust mark. Like I said, tedious…. It's worth the effort, though.

3. Before you get down to all of that hard work, though, you might want to try the Despeckle filter (choose Image, Noise, Despeckle). The Despeckle filter can remove some of the smaller spots and reduce the work you have to do manually.

Figure 17.3 is the result of running the Despeckle filter on the image.

FIGURE 17.3.

The Despeckle filter removes most of the dust spots.

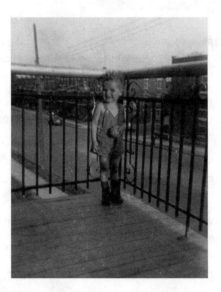

Figure 17.4 is the result of removing all but the worst (the largest) of the remaining spots.

FIGURE 17.4.

The rest of the spots removed manually with the Dropper and Paint Brushes tools.

17

Any remaining marks, such as the scratches, will have to be removed with the Clone Brush tool. As you may recall from Hour 8, "Painting Tools and Techniques," the Clone Brush tool (which resembles two brushes together) copies one portion of an image over another.

You select the portion you want to copy by right-clicking and then clicking-and-dragging to copy the area you've selected over another area. As you draw with the Clone Brush tool, you'll see two cursors: One cursor shows you where you're copying from, and one shows you where you're copying to.

As with the Dropper/Paint Brushes combination, you should constantly change where you're copying from by right-clicking in a new area.

A word of caution: When you work with the Clone Brush tool, even though you've changed the areas that you're cloning and you've moved over the entire image you're working on, choosing Edit, Undo will undo *all* the work that you've done.

I highly recommend saving periodically. You can save the image as Image01, Image02, Image03, and so on. But if you don't save and you need to undo a step, you'll end up undoing all of your cloning work. Of course, you can Edit, Redo, but you won't be able to Undo the very last boo-boo you made.

As with the Dropper/Paint Brushes combination, you'll want to zoom in to get a clear view of the areas that need work. You'll also want to adjust the Clone Brush settings in the same manner as you adjusted the Paint Brushes tool. That is, you'll want a fairly small, soft, slightly transparent brush. Remember, you're correcting an existing image, not painting a new one.

You'll also want to keep changing the area you're cloning from, depending on the area you want to cover. Just right-click when you want to select a new area and keep working.

Figure 17.5 is the result after using the Clone Brush tool on some of the worst marks.

FIGURE 17.5.

The worst marks were removed manually with the Clone Brush tool.

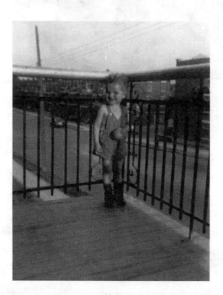

Compare Figure 17.5 to the original image in Figure 17.1. Quite an improvement already, but there's more. The final touch-up is to sharpen the image with the Unsharp Mask filter.

Using the Unsharp Mask Filter

To fix the sharpness, or lack thereof, I'll use the Unsharp Mask filter. The Unsharp Mask filter mimics a traditional film compositing technique used to sharpen the edges of an image.

The Unsharp Mask works by increasing the contrast between adjacent pixels. The edges it works on are based on the difference of the pixels in the image using the values you enter for the different options. All of this sounds complex, and it is. Using the filter is not as complex, though.

To apply the Unsharp Mask, choose Image, Sharpen, Unsharp Mask. Doing so brings up the Unsharp Mask dialog box (see Figure 17.6).

FIGURE 17.6.

The Unsharp Mask dialog box and the image to which the filter is being applied.

17

Aside from the usual Zoom, Auto Proof, and preview options, you'll see three different options that you can set: Radius, Strength, and Clipping.

- The Radius setting determines how many pixels in an area will be affected by the filter. As this number increases, so does the apparent sharpness of the image. Setting too high a number, though, simply increases the overall contrast of the image, especially if you also increase the Strength setting.

- The Strength setting affects how much the contrast will change over the areas affected by the filter. Setting this number too high simply makes the image appear to have too much contrast.

- The Clipping setting is important. This option determines how much contrast must exist between the pixels before the filter will be applied to an area. If "dust marks" show up as you lower this value, you'll want to adjust it a little higher.

Basically, the values you enter depend on a particular image and the results you're after. I used 2.00 for the Radius setting, 100% for the Strength setting, and 3 for the Clipping value to arrive at the final, retouched image shown in Figure 17.7.

FIGURE 17.7.

*The final retouched
image with the con-
trast improved, all of
the dust marks and
scratches removed,
and the sharpness
corrected.*

Compare this image to the original in Figure 17.1, and I'm sure you'll agree that it's a big improvement. This image could now be printed and hanged.

Retouching to Remove Portions of an Image

As well as retouching older images, you may simply need to work on an area of a photograph to change some portion of the image. You may want to remove someone's braces, for example, or make minor corrections to a person's complexion.

Retouching tricks such as these are certainly possible with Paint Shop Pro. Figure 17.8 shows a close-up of a portrait where the model is still wearing braces.

FIGURE 17.8.

*Portrait with braces
showing.*

You can correct this lovely smile by using some of the same techniques you used to retouch the old photo in the previous exercise.

To remove some of the smaller offending areas, you can use the Dropper/Paint Brushes technique.

Remember to lower the opacity of the Paint Brushes tool so that you gradually cover an area as you work, rather than trying to speed things up by quickly painting over an area. Better to work an area over several times than to make too large an adjustment that glaringly shows that the image has been retouched.

The whole idea is to do the retouching in a way that fools the viewer into believing that the image is in its pristine original condition. Try using a "light hand" in the form of smaller, softer, more transparent brushes.

Figure 17.9 shows the results of using the Dropper/Paint Brushes technique to remove the braces on the bottom teeth and at the sides of the mouth.

17

FIGURE 17.9.

Initial retouching with the Dropper/Paint Brushes technique removes some of the braces.

I think that's about as far as the Dropper/Paint Brushes technique will carry me, though. It's time for the Clone Brush tool.

Using the Clone Brush tool, I can copy portions of the teeth where there are no braces over areas where the braces exist. Again, working with the Clone Brush tool, it's wise to make frequent backups.

You'll also want to constantly change the area that you're cloning from so that you don't just copy large areas over existing areas. Doing so would be a dead giveaway that the image had been retouched.

Sometimes, you'll unavoidably make a bit of a mess of an area with the Clone Brush tool. Don't panic, though. Here's a trick you can use to help fix some of those problem areas.

Figure 17.10 shows one such area caused by overworking the Clone Brush tool. You can see how the front tooth that I've been working on is slightly speckled.

FIGURE **17.10.**

Problem area caused by overworking the Clone Brush tool.

To fix this area, select the Freehand tool and set the feathering value to 2 or so. Use the Freehand tool to select the offending area (see Figure 17.11).

FIGURE **17.11.**

Problem area selected with the Freehand tool.

With the area selected, choose the Gaussian Blur filter (Image, Blur, Gaussian Blur) and turn on the Auto Proof option. Adjust the Radius setting until the area is corrected.

What you're going for is the removal of the marks made with the Clone Brush tool while maintaining the same graininess and appearance as the surrounding image.

Figure 17.12 shows the Gaussian Blur dialog box with the settings I used and the results of the application of the blur on the image.

FIGURE 17.12.

Problem area corrected with the application of the Gaussian Blur filter.

Figure 17.13 shows the image with the braces totally removed from the portrait.

FIGURE 17.13.

Braces totally removed from the portrait.

17

A few problem areas remain. The retouching has left some of the areas of the teeth a little darker than they should be. Fortunately, this defect is easy to correct.

To lighten up the areas that were darkened with the Clone Brush tool, I selected the Retouch tool (it resembles a small hand with one finger pointing downward). Again, I set a soft brush with a low opacity setting (these options are in the Controls palette). I set the Tool Controls to Lighten RGB and moved the brush around the offending area.

> The Retouch tool can be used to selectively change areas of an image. You can choose to lighten, darken, soften, sharpen, emboss, smudge, push, dodge and burn (*dodge* and *burn* are photographic darkroom terms meaning lighten and darken), saturation up, saturation down, lightness up, lightness down, hue up, hue down, saturation to target, lightness to target, hue to target, and color to target. That's a lot of options!
>
> Once you've selected the Retouch tool and set the Retouch mode, you can adjust the Brush Tip, as I've done in this exercise, to retouch small areas of the image.

As I worked, I changed the brush size and worked lightly over the areas I wanted to lighten. Figure 17.14 shows the final braceless smile.

FIGURE 17.14.

Final retouched smile.

Perfect!

Work like this takes time and practice. Done properly, though, it's certainly worth the effort.

Summary

This hour was a bit tough. Don't stop here, though. Retouching photographs is an art form that requires lots of time and practice to get right. As you can see from the results, it's worth the time and effort.

As with any other art form, you'll get better with practice. I've shown you a couple of tricks and a shortcut or two. The rest is up to you. If you have images that are in need of work, get them out and start playing around with the techniques I've described. You'll be amazed at the results.

Before getting back into some more of the fun stuff, I tackle one more difficult subject in the next hour: coloring and color correction.

Workshop

17

The workshop contains a question and answer section to help answer the most commonly asked questions and quiz questions to help you solidify your understanding of the material covered.

Q&A

Q I'm not clear on why you lower the opacity of the brushes when retouching. Can you explain why you do so?

A I lower the opacity to change the amount of effect a brush has. I'd rather apply a subtle effect two or three times than apply an obvious (or overdone) effect once. Lowering the opacity of the brush enables me to make a less obvious retouch.

Q Why do you use such a small brush size when retouching?

A Again, it's a matter of subtlety. What you're trying to do is retouch an image without the image appearing to have been retouched. Making smaller changes as you work enables you to make the changes less obvious.

Q Why do you keep changing the settings of the various tools as you work?

A It's still that subtlety thing. A digital image contains many small pixels of varying color and luminance. Large sweeping changes are usually obvious to anyone who views your work. Changing the size, opacity, and other variables as you work makes the changes far less obvious. With enough practice, the changes will be virtually invisible to anyone who views the results of your work.

Quiz

1. What's a quick way to remove the many small dust marks that may be present on an older image?

2. How do you remove the remaining dust marks?

3. Is there a trick that can help when the Clone Brush tool makes a bit of a mess of an area?

4. Can a graphics tablet help with retouching?

Answers

1. You can use the Despeckle filter (choose Image, Noise, Despeckle) to remove most of the smaller dust marks.

2. You can use the Dropper/Paint Brushes technique. This process involves switching between the two tools, picking up nearby colors with the Dropper, and applying them with the Paint Brushes tool.

3. Yes. You can make a freehand, feathered selection and run the Gaussian Blur filter on the area.

4. Yes. As with other digital imaging, a tablet is a much better tool than a mouse.

Hour 18

Coloring and Color Correction

Discussing color in a black-and-white book may seem silly. However, most of the work you do with Paint Shop Pro will be in color, and just because I can't show you color examples doesn't mean that I can't tell you how to use color in your work.

This hour tackles the following issues related to color:

- Understanding the theory behind good color
- Understanding gamma correction
- Adjusting the hue, saturation, and lightness
- Working with the Map Hue command
- Adjusting the reds, greens, and blues in your color
- Grasping color correction in a nutshell

A Little Color Theory

Color on a computer screen is somewhat different from color in other media such as finger paints. You may remember back to when, as a child, you would mix a couple of primary colors to get a secondary color. For example, you might mix blue and yellow to get green, right?

Well, the idea is the same when it comes to the colors you see on your computer screen. The biggest difference is that the colors you worked with as a child were red, yellow, and blue, and the colors you'll use for digital work are red, green, and blue.

Here's how it works. If you mix two of the three colors from the choices of red, green, and blue, you'll get cyan, magenta, or yellow.

Sound familiar? You may recall that cyan, magenta, and yellow make up the CMYK color model (used for printing). Forget that for now, though. We'll be concentrating on the color scheme you see on your screen, which is the RGB color model.

To see how the colors mix, take a look at Michael's Modified Color Wheel (see Figure 18.1).

FIGURE 18.1.

Michael's Modified Color Wheel.

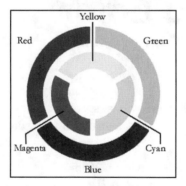

If you take any two of the colors from the outside of the wheel and mix them, you get the color on the inside between the two that you mixed.

Conversely, if you take any two colors from the inside of the wheel and add them, you'll get the color from the outside between the two that you mixed.

Also, the opposite of any color is on the other wheel. In other words, if you want to know the opposite of green, find green on the wheel and then find its opposite on the other wheel. Green is on the outside, so its opposite color is across from it on the inside. Therefore, the opposite of green is magenta.

This system tells you, the digital artist, what colors to add to an image to correct any color cast caused by bad scans, bad photo finishing, and so on. For example, if an image is too green, simply add magenta to correct it.

How much magenta? It really depends on the image. There is no magic formula.

On the other hand, Paint Shop Pro has many tools to help you correct color problems with your images. In fact, some of Paint Shop Pro's color tools make it easy to correct an image's color faults by enabling you to subtract from a color rather than worry about which color to add, and most of them work in the Hue, Saturation, Lightness (HSL) or RGB models.

The first thing you might need to adjust in an image is the brightness and contrast. Rather than immediately going for the Brightness/Contrast option, though, you should consider one other option: gamma correction.

Understanding Gamma Correction

An image's *gamma* is a combination of its brightness and contrast. Consequently, you can adjust both the brightness and the contrast by simply adjusting the gamma.

The Gamma Correction option does a nice job of correcting the brightness and contrast of a color image. Using the Brightness/Contrast option throws away too many shades and/or colors, in effect leaving gaps in the histogram (discussed shortly) of an image.

Using the Gamma Correction Feature

To use the Gamma Correction feature, choose Colors, Adjust, Gamma Correction. Figure 18.2 shows the Gamma Correction dialog box, along with an image having its gamma adjusted.

FIGURE 18.2.

An image having its gamma adjusted.

18

To lighten an image, drag the sliders to the right. To darken an image, drag the sliders to the left.

If the overall image needs to be lightened or darkened, leave the sliders linked. If you want to change the gamma of only one color, unlink the sliders by toggling the Link option off and then moving the slider for that particular color (see Figure 18.3).

FIGURE 18.3.

An image having its green channel's gamma adjusted.

The photograph I was working on still had a bit of a green cast to it that was easily corrected by unlinking the sliders and adjusting the green slider to the left.

Using the Histogram Palette

With many images, small changes to the gamma will suffice. However, sometimes more drastic changes are needed. How can you tell when an image needs adjusting and where it needs to be adjusted? That's where the Histogram palette comes in.

To see the histogram, click on the Histogram icon. It resembles a small black-and-white bar graph and is located in the standard toolbar. You can use the histogram to see how the colors and the luminance of your image are distributed. Figure 18.4 is the histogram of the image before I started to work on it.

You can see right away that the image is too dark. The histogram verifies this impression in that the graphs don't go all the way to the right. A good image has a more even distribution in the histogram.

If the histogram graph is higher towards the right, too much of a certain color is present or the image is too light, depending on which graph you're examining.

FIGURE 18.4.

An image that needs correcting and its histogram.

If the graph is bunched up towards the left, you have too little of the color that is represented or the image is too dark.

Figure 18.5 is the same image as Figure 18.4 after the gamma corrections.

FIGURE 18.5.

An image that has been corrected and its histogram.

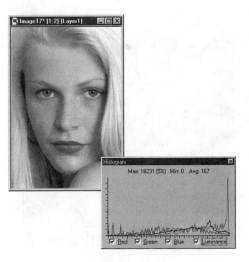

18

Did you notice the better distribution of the graphs in the histogram? The graphs all go to the right now, and more of the graphs can be seen. This change in the histogram is a result of the changes made to the image with the Gamma Correction tool.

You can use the histogram to "read" an image's color cast, as well. If one graph is way off in relationship to the others, you'll know that the image has a color cast in that particular color.

Several menu items are associated with the histogram. You can either equalize or stretch a histogram:

- The Equalize command smoothes out the histogram so that the image's brightness is averaged.
- The Stretch command stretches the histogram so that the brightness of an image is spread more broadly across the histogram.

Both of these options are available under Colors, Histogram Functions. These commands have limited capabilities, though. If an image is really bad, they'll have almost no effect.

Playing with Other Color Adjustments

After setting an image's gamma, you can move on to making more color adjustments if necessary.

For example, you can adjust the highlights, midtones, and shadows separately with the Highlight/Midtone/Shadow command (choose Colors, Adjust, Highlight/Midtone/Shadow—see Figure 18.6).

FIGURE 18.6.

Adjusting an image's highlights, midtones, and shadows.

The highlights in an image are the lighter areas, the shadows are the darker areas, and the midtones are the areas in between. This idea may seem a little simplistic, but it basically reflects those areas in an image. In a black-and-white photo, the highlights are the light greys and the whites, the shadows are the dark greys and blacks, and the other middle grey areas are the midtones.

Moving the sliders to the right lightens the highlights, the midtones, or the shadows; moving them to the left darkens the highlights, midtones, or shadows.

As with any of the other color adjustment commands, you'll want to move the sliders in very small increments. Large movements will distort your image.

Adjusting the Hue, Saturation, and Lightness

You can also adjust an image's hue (or color cast), saturation (or amount of overall color), and lightness (overall brightness).

To do so, choose Colors, Adjust, Hue/Saturation/Lightness to bring up the Hue/Saturation/Lightness dialog box (see Figure 18.7).

FIGURE 18.7.

Adjusting an image's hue, saturation, and lightness.

In Figure 18.7, I've lowered the saturation and raised the lightness a little to give the photograph the appearance of a hi-key image.

A *hi-key image* is an image, or photograph, that is very light. You'll see hi-key photographs used a lot in magazine ads for women's cosmetics.

You can get some cool effects with your photographs with this command. You can, for example, lower the saturation to the point where the color is barely there. This look would be similar to the effect of a hand-colored photograph.

Working with the Map Hue Command

The Map Hue command is very powerful because it enables you to completely remap, or change, any color into any other. With the Hue Map, colors are described in terms of degrees around the color wheel seen in the Color dialog box (not Michael's Modified Color Wheel).

If you take a look at the Map Hue dialog box in Figure 18.8 (choose Colors, Adjust, Hue Map), you'll notice that numbers are associated with each of the 10 color sliders.

FIGURE 18.8.

The Map Hue dialog box.

The numbers go up in increments of 36 from 0 degrees to 324 degrees. Each color occupies 36 degrees.

This is the way that colors are mapped to the color wheel when you look at colors expressed as HSL.

As you change the settings of a color slider, you'll see a change in the image preview window (the right-most preview window), which you can compare to the unmodified image (in the small preview window to the left). You can also control the saturation and lightness shifts from the Map Hue dialog box. Remember that small changes are best.

Take a look at the color wheel in the Color dialog box (see Figure 18.9), and you'll see how the colors are arranged around the wheel.

FIGURE 18.9.

The Color dialog box.

At this point you may be viewing the color wheel in a whole new light. If you measured the colors around the wheel in terms of degrees, you'd see how neatly the colors fit onto the wheel.

Getting back to the Map Hue command, you can, as I said, remap any color to any other color. You will want to make these adjustments in very small increments, though, unless you plan on creating strange effects from your photographs.

To remap any color to any other, simply move the slider up or down until you achieve the change you want.

Adjusting the Reds, Greens, and Blues of Your Image

The last choice in the Colors, Adjust menu is the Red, Green, and Blue command. This command enables you to separately change the red, green, and blue values in an image.

As with the other dialog boxes, you'll find a real-time preview, an Auto Proof checkbox, and the sliders that enable you to change the different values for the red, green, and blue in your image (see Figure 18.10).

You'll want to use the same amount of caution when moving these sliders as you will with the others. Even a change of 3 or 4 can make a visible difference in your image.

18

FIGURE 18.10.

The Red/Green/Blue dialog box.

You can easily remove a color cast by entering negative values into the sliders in the Red/Green/Blue dialog box.

For example, my original image was a little green, and I adjusted it by entering –3 for the Green value in the Red/Green/Blue dialog box.

I obviously can't show you the results here, but that small change fixed the slight green cast that resulted from the photo-finishing process.

Color Correction in a Nutshell

To recap, the first thing you should do after acquiring your image is adjust the gamma. This step enables you to lighten or darken and change the contrast without affecting the histogram as much as the Brightness/Contrast command would.

You can test this yourself by loading an image and duplicating it with Edit, Copy and then Edit, Paste as New Image (or press Shift+D) so that you have two images open concurrently. Then follow these steps:

1. Check the number of colors in the image by choosing Colors, Count Colors Used.

2. Turn on the Histogram palette and change one image with the Brightness/Contrast command (Colors, Adjust, Brightness) and change the other using the Gamma Correction command (Colors Adjust, Gamma Correction).

You may find that the Brightness/Contrast command compresses the histogram, whereas the Gamma Correction command does not. You may also find, by checking the number of colors in each image, that the number of colors is significantly lower after the application of the Brightness/Contrast command as compared to the application of the Gamma Correction command.

3. When you've corrected the overall gamma, you can unlink the sliders and, if necessary, change the gamma of the colors separately.

4. If your image is still in need of some help, you can examine the histogram again. The histogram should, depending on the particular image, show a nice even distribution of all of the colors and the luminance.

   Recall that if the graph is higher towards the right, too much of a certain color is present or the image is too light, depending on which graph you're examining. If the graph is bunched up towards the left, you have too little of the color that is represented or the image is too dark.

5. If the gamma correction isn't helping, you can make further adjustments with either the RGB command or the HSL command (Colors, Adjust, RGB or Colors, Adjust, HSL). You'll want to make these changes in very small increments, though.

6. By adding or subtracting to the Hue, Saturation, and Lightness or the Red, Green, and Blue sliders in the HSL or RGB dialog box, you'll be able to make the final adjustments necessary to bring your image into line.

Color and color correction are incredibly complex subjects, requiring much time, patience, and study. Many professionals have spent their lifetimes studying these subjects.

If it doesn't seem easy as you start out, don't get too frustrated. With time and practice, you'll certainly be able to adjust your photographs so that they display properly. Most of the time, it's a matter of trial and error—don't forget to use the Undo command!

Summary

This tough hour presented some theory and even more options. You'll want to spend some time playing with the different commands to see what effect they have on your images. Correcting an image's color is even more difficult than retouching and will require much time, effort, and practice. One day, though, you'll be able to look at a high-priced magazine ad and wonder why someone didn't add just a little more red.

With the two toughest subjects in digital imaging out of the way, it's time to get back to the fun stuff. In the next hour, I show you how to composite two or more images together. This high-end technique can produce amazing images.

Workshop

The workshop contains a question and answer section to help answer the most commonly asked questions and quiz questions to help you solidify your understanding of the material covered.

Q&A

Q How is HSL different from RGB?

A HSL and RGB are just two different ways of looking at the same thing—the color wheel. If you check the RGB and HSL settings in the Color dialog box, you'll see that each RGB has a corresponding HSL and vice versa.

Q How would you fix a green tint in a photograph?

A You could lower the green using Colors, Adjust, Red/Green/Blue.

Q How do you replace color hues?

A You can do so via the Hue Map (choose Colors, Adjust, Hue Map).

Quiz

1. Using Figure 18.1 as your guide, what color would you need to add to an image that had too much cyan in it?

2. What does a histogram of an image tell you about the distribution of color within the image? What does it mean if the histogram graph is higher towards the right side?

3. What is the difference between the RGB and HSL color models?

4. What does the Map Hue command do for you?

Answers

1. You would need to add red to compensate for the cyan tint.

2. The histogram reflects the distribution of color and light in an image. A histogram that is weighted too far to the right indicates too much of a certain color or an image that's too light, depending on which graph you're reading.

3. The only difference is in the way that a color is represented. It's like reading a book in one language and then reading it again in another language. It's the same book, but with a different way of looking at it.

4. It enables you to replace one hue (or color) with another.

18

Hour 19

Compositing

Compositing is the art of merging photographs together. There are two basic styles of compositing. The first style—called a *collage*—places images together in a way that makes it obvious that the images are from different sources. This technique is currently very popular. You see collages in magazines and television ads every day. The second style of compositing is the *photo montage* or just *montage*. With a montage, the trick is to fool the viewers into believing that what they're seeing is real, even though it's impossible. Examples of this type of composite are flying cars, people placed into older images that might have been taken before they were even born, and so on.

This hour tackles the following issues related to composites:

- Creating collages
- Creating photo montages

Creating Collages

Creating a collage is easier than creating a montage because you're not trying to fool the viewer. What you want to accomplish with a collage is a nice composition using different images. In doing so, you hope to convey a message of some sort.

Before you start a collage, you should gather your source material and decide on the general layout that will convey your idea. In this exercise, I construct a fictitious brochure for a railway company; the brochure's purpose is to entice the viewer to ride the rails.

To get started, I selected three images of trains that I thought would work well together in the brochure. Figures 19.1 through 19.3 are the three images I selected.

FIGURE 19.1.

Photograph of a railway switch.

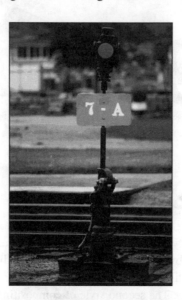

FIGURE 19.2.

Photograph of a locomotive engine.

FIGURE 19.3.

A close-up of a train's wheels.

I've already resized the images a little so that they all more or less share the same dimensions.

To resize the images after scanning them, you choose Image, Resize. The Resize dialog box (see Figure 19.4) has all of the necessary options to help you resize an image.

FIGURE 19.4.

Paint Shop Pro's Resize dialog box.

19

To begin, you should decide on the approximate size for the final, or composite, image and set the dimensions for the first, or base, image on which the other images will be placed.

Because the Resize dialog box remembers the last dimensions you used, it's relatively easy to set the new size for the remaining images. This statement is true, even though the third image (train wheels) is in landscape mode (wider than it is high), whereas the other two are in portrait mode (higher than they are wide).

When it came to resizing the train wheels image, I just used the Width setting of the first two images. The Resize dialog box enables you to keep the proportions of the image (by placing a checkmark in the Maintain Aspect Ratio Of checkbox) so after setting the width, I just clicked OK and the image was set to the proper size.

After resizing the image, the next step is to place copies of the second and third images into new layers in the first image. You can follow the next sequence of steps with any three images—just modify the discussion for your own images. Follow these steps to create your collage:

1. Select the second image (the engine) and choose Edit, Copy to copy the entire image to the Clipboard.

2. Make the first image current by clicking its title bar.

3. Choose Edit, Paste, As New Layer. You don't need the second image for now, so go ahead and close it.

4. To copy the third image onto the first as a new layer, repeat the above process.

5. At this point, you should have one image with three layers (similar to Figure 19.5).

FIGURE 19.5.

Multilayered image ready to be turned into a collage.

You can see that I've renamed the layers just to keep things easier to manage. You can rename them by double-clicking each layer's name in turn in the Layers palette and renaming it.

6. Now you need to blend the second layer into the first. To help with this process, you can turn off the visibility of the top layer (the one with the wheels). It'll still be there, it just won't be visible. To turn off a layer's visibility, simply click the Layer Visibility Toggle icon in the Layers palette.

7. To help me resize and place the engine, I'll reduce its layer's opacity so that I can see through to the layer below. To do so, I can simply adjust the opacity with the slider in the Layers palette.

8. To resize the image of the engine, select the entire layer (Selections, Select All) and then select the Deformation tool. (It's the rectangular-shaped icon and is the third from the top if your Tool palette is placed vertically and third from the left if horizontally.)

   I used the Deformation tool to resize the engine layer so that it would fit into the upper-left corner of the image (see Figure 19.6).

FIGURE **19.6.**

The engine resized and moved into the upper-left corner.

9. I'd like to fade the edges of the Engine layer to make the collage flow more easily. To do so, I selected an oval area around the engine with the Selection tool style set to Elliptical and the Feather value set to about 6.

10. Copy the selection to the Clipboard (Edit, Copy) and then paste the selection to its own layer (Edit, Paste, As New Layer).

    This step enables you to have a copy of the entire Engine layer if you decide to change the selection in some way.

11. To continue, turn off the visibility of the original Engine layer and move the elliptical selection into place (see Figure 19.7).

    With the selection in place, choose Selections, Select None.

FIGURE 19.7.

The engine fit into a feathered elliptical shape.

I want the switch to show through the engine a little more than it does, though. The answer is to use a mask to change the opacity of the engine and let the switch show through.

12. To create the mask, use Masks, New, Show All. To see the mask as you work on it, choose Masks, View Mask. I then chose Masks, Edit to work on the mask. All that's left now is to paint the mask in.

    Painting in black will add to the mask and let the image below show through, whereas painting in white will bring back any areas you've masked out.

13. After painting in the mask, I decided that the engine was too small. To fix the problem I chose Masks, Delete and deleted the mask. (Note that a dialog box pops up when you choose to delete the mask—I was deleting the mask because of an error, so I chose not to merge the current mask.) I then used the Deformation tool to resize the engine so that it was a bit larger. I then redrew the mask (sometimes it's a matter of trial and error).

Figure 19.8 shows the engine and its mask in place.

Time to add the wheels. Remember that the wheels are already there on a separate layer; they've just had their layer's visibility turned off. To turn on the layer's visibility, simply toggle the Layer Visibility Toggle icon in the Layers palette.

FIGURE 19.8.

The engine and its mask in place.

1. I want the wheels at the bottom of the collage with the background slowly blending into them. To accomplish this blend, I first moved the wheels into place at the bottom of the image using the Mover tool—its icon resembles a cross with arrow heads (see Figure 19.9).

FIGURE 19.9.

The Wheels layer moved into place and its visibility turned back on.

19

2. To select the wheels so I could create the mask, I used the Magic Wand and selected the transparent area above the wheels. I then inverted the selection with Selections, Invert.

3. To create the new mask, choose Masks, New, Show Selection.

4. Choose Masks, Edit so that you can add a gradient fill to the mask.

5. To fill the mask with the gradient, select the Flood Fill tool and set the Type option to Linear Gradient.

6. Set the foreground color to black and the background color to white.

7. Set the gradient direction to 180 degrees and then click in the selected area to fill the mask with a black-to-white linear gradient.

8. To turn off the editing and the view of the mask, choose Masks, Edit and Masks, View Masks.

Figure 19.10 shows the final collage.

FIGURE 19.10.

The final collage created in Paint Shop Pro.

All that's needed to turn this into a brochure is some text, as shown in Figure 19.11.

To add text, select the Text tool, place the mouse pointer where you want the text to appear in the image, and click. You then enter your text in the Text dialog box. Remember also that you should add text to a new layer so that you can change the text without redoing the entire image.

FIGURE 19.11.

*The final brochure with
the text in place.*

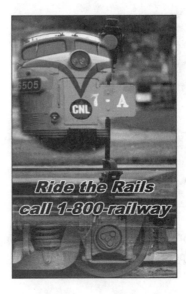

I show you how I created the outlined text effect in the next hour.

Creating Photo Montages

Creating photo montages is a more complex process, or it can be under certain circumstances. I create a relatively simple photo montage in the next exercise, and along the way I point out things that you should watch for when creating your own.

Figures 19.12 and 19.13 are the two images I'll be compositing in this exercise.

FIGURE 19.12.

A graffiti-covered wall.

19

FIGURE 19.13.

A self-portrait of the author shot in his studio.

Figure 19.12 is an outdoor shot of a graffiti-covered wall. The original was shot on color slide film. Figure 19.13 is a self-portrait of the author (that would be me) taken in the studio and shot on black-and-white film.

Your modus operandi when creating photo montages is to eliminate all differences between the photos so that they appear to be from the same image. You'll have to adjust the images in several areas ("gotchas"): lighting, shadows, film speed, size, and color, to name a few.

The first gotcha here would be that the two films are different: One is color slide film, and the other is black-and-white negative film. An easy way around this problem, of course, is to convert the color slide to black and white (or "greyscale," as it's called in digital imaging) after scanning it into Paint Shop Pro.

To convert the color photo into greyscale, choose Colors, Gray Scale. You should remember to bump the color resolution back up afterward. To do so, choose Colors, Increase Color Depth, 16 Million Colors.

For the montage to work, the self-portrait needed a little resizing after it was scanned in so that both images would be the same size relative to each other. The process here is the same as that discussed earlier with the train images.

Essentially, what I want to do is superimpose the studio shot onto the location shot of the graffiti-covered wall. The first step is to isolate the self-portrait:

1. In this particular case, the solid-colored background of the studio simplifies the isolation process.

   With the background one solid-color, I simply used the Magic Wand to select the background and then inverted the selection (Selections, Invert) to select the self-portrait.

If this image showed the subject against other objects, the process of selecting the subject would be more involved and would require the techniques shown in Hour 12, "Masks."

2. When the subject is selected, copy it to the Clipboard (Edit, Copy) and paste it into a new layer on the Graffiti image.

3. To paste the selection into the Graffiti image, make the Graffiti image current and then choose Edit, Paste, As New Layer (see Figure 19.14).

FIGURE 19.14.

The subject from Figure 19.13 pasted into the image from Figure 19.12.

Because the subject is on its own layer, moving it into place with the Mover tool is a simple matter (see Figure 19.15).

19

FIGURE 19.15.

The subject from Figure 19.13 moved into place.

Even though these photographs were shot on different types of film, they were both shot with the same ISO (that is, they were both shot with film of the same speed). The lighting in both photographs is also similar enough to not be a problem. If either of these variables is a problem with the images you're trying to composite, though, you may have to consider reshooting.

4. Now you must fix the differences in the photos, such as lighting, shadows, and film speed, to produce a more realistic effect. The only difference in the photos here is that the background should be a little fuzzier than the subject to mimic the effect of distance in a photograph. That situation is easily corrected by running the Gaussian Blur filter against the background image, though.

Figure 19.16 shows the final montage.

FIGURE 19.16.

The subject has been moved to make a better composition, and some Gaussian Blur was added to the background.

Creating montages is an art form and requires much time, patience, and practice. But it's something that you can have fun with, too.

I've barely scratched the surface of what can be done with these techniques. In fact, whole books have been written on the subject. For more information, try *Photoshop Collage Techniques* by Gregory Cosmo Haun. This book is published by Hayden, and its ISBN is 1-56830-349-1.

Summary

This enjoyable hour mixed theory and practice. I hope I've given you some ideas of what you can do with photographs, Paint Shop Pro, and some time and effort. I doubt that you'll be able to look at printed photos in the same way anymore, knowing the magic that can be accomplished with a digital imaging program such as Paint Shop Pro.

In the next hour, I show you how to create more special effects using combinations of filters and other tools.

Workshop

The workshop contains a question and answer section to help answer the most commonly asked questions and quiz questions to help you solidify your understanding of the material covered.

Q&A

Q How do I resize an image without changing its relative dimensions?

A The Resize dialog box has a checkbox called Maintain Aspect Ratio. Placing a checkmark in this checkbox maintains the relative dimensions of an image as you resize it.

Q Can I create an image using both the montage and collage techniques?

A Yes, you could. Of course, the resulting image would be seen as a collage because of the collage elements in it.

Q What tricks can I use to align or correct shadow differences in an image?

A If the sun was on one side in one image and on the other in the other image, one trick would be to flip one of the images. This technique can have its drawbacks, though. If, for example, the image that you flip has text, it would be readily apparent to the viewer and might spoil the illusion. Some shadows might be very difficult, if not impossible, to fix. In such cases, you might want to consider reshooting the photo.

Quiz

1. Explain the difference between a collage and a montage.

2. When creating a collage in Paint Shop Pro, what happens after resizing your images?

3. Why would you want to turn off a layer's visibility while creating a collage? How do you do this?

19

4. Why is creating a montage usually a more complicated task than creating a collage?

Answers

1. A collage is a collection of images placed together using layers and masks so that the final image appears to be created from several images. A montage is also built of several images; however, the objective is to fool the viewer into believing that the image was actually shot on one frame of film, even if the subject matter is unbelievable.

2. The next step after adding each image to a separate layer and resizing it is to place each layer to get a rough idea of the layout or composition.

3. Turning a layer's visibility on and off helps to cut down on some of the visual static. Sometimes working with less visual information is easier than working with visibility turned on.

4. With a montage, you're trying to fool the viewer into believing that the final image is real and not digitally created.

Hour 20

Combining Advanced Techniques/Spectacular Examples

Sometimes the difference between a good effect and a great one is simply adding another effect over one that's already present. Other times, you can get a special effect just by trying something that you normally wouldn't think of.

In this hour, I show you how to use some Paint Shop Pro tools in ways you might not have thought of. I cover the following advanced techniques:

- Outlining text and other objects
- Filling text with textures or photos
- Creating an interface

Outlining Text and Other Objects

One technique that Paint Shop Pro doesn't offer is a way to outline objects. You can, of course, outline rectangles, squares, circles, and ellipses when you create them, but there's no easy way to outline some odd-shaped object such as text. Or is there?

In Hour 19, "Compositing," you may have noticed the 1-800 number on the final railway brochure (Figure 19.11) and wondered how I did that. Here's how:

1. Open a new 600×300 image with the resolution set to 72 pixels per inch, the background color set to white, and the image type set to 16.7 million colors.

2. Add a new layer for the text, by clicking the Add New Layer icon at the bottom of the Layers palette, and name it **Text**. You'll need to add the new layer because you'll be adding another layer later that will go between the layer with your text and the Background layer.

3. Set the foreground color to the color you want your text to be. I chose a pale blue.

4. Use the Text tool to add some text to your image. I added the word **Outlined** in 90-point Arial Black.

   The text should still be selected—it should still have the marquee around it.

5. Make the Background layer active by clicking its name in the Layers palette. This technique is a quick way of having the new layer appear above the Background layer and the Text layer. Alternatively, you can create the new layer and click-and-drag it into place.

6. Add another new layer and name it **Outline**.

7. Choose Selections, Modify, Expand and enter a value of **5**.

   You should now have three layers: the Background layer, a layer with an active selection called Outline, and another layer on top called Text (see Figure 20.1).

FIGURE 20.1.

Background, expanded selection, and text.

8. With the Outline layer active, set the foreground color to the color you want for the outline. I chose black as the outline color for this exercise.

9. Select the Flood Fill tool (it resembles a small paint bucket tipped over slightly) and click inside the selection. You may have to use this technique in several areas to fill the entire outline.

10. Choose Selections, Select None, and you should have text that resembles that shown in Figure 20.2.

FIGURE 20.2.

Outlined text.

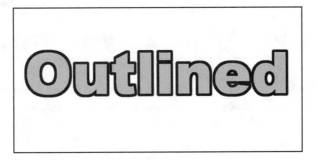

You can use this technique to outline anything that you can select. In fact, I use a similar technique to outline multiple objects in vector programs such as Illustrator. Figure 20.3 is an example of this popular illustration effect.

FIGURE 20.3.

Pen with dark outline shown in Illustrator.

20

You can also expand on this technique and have the text in white on a white background so that the text would appear as just the outline (see Figure 20.4).

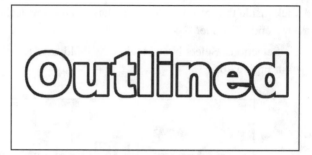

This technique gives the appearance that the text is outlined and doesn't have anything in its center. I accomplished this effect using exactly the same steps as explained previously except that the text is white instead of blue.

Filling Text with Textures or Photos

You can use the effect described in the last section to fill the text with a texture or even a photo and outline it. Here's how:

1. Start with two photographs. I'm using two photographs of fall leaves (see Figures 20.5 and 20.6).

2. Make the image that you want to place the text onto active by clicking its title bar.
3. Add a new layer to this image and name it **Text**.

4. Use the Text tool to add some text.

5. Leave the text selected and select the Flood Fill tool.

FIGURE 20.6.

Red fall leaves.

6. Under the Controls tab in the Controls palette, set the Fill Style option to Pattern.

7. Click Options to bring up the Flood Fill Options dialog box.

8. Use the New Pattern Source pull-down menu to choose the red leaves as the pattern source. This step will enable you to fill the text selection with the red leaves.

9. One by one, click the letters so that they become filled with the image pattern (see Figure 20.7).

FIGURE 20.7.

Letters on one image filled with the pattern of another.

20

To make the letters more visible, you can use the same techniques as I did in the previous example:

1. With the text still selected, create a new layer above the Background layer.
2. Expand the selection by choosing Selections, Modify, Expand. This time I used a value of 3.
3. Set the foreground to white and click in each letter to fill it with white. Make sure that you've reset the Fill Style to Solid Color under the Controls tab in the Controls palette.
4. Choose Selections, Select None.

You should have something similar to the image in Figure 20.8.

FIGURE 20.8.

Outlined letters on one image filled with the pattern of another.

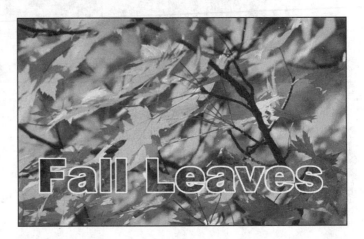

Creating an Interface

The next technique uses some of the techniques you've already learned, along with a couple of new tricks.

This project demonstrates the step-by-step process that goes into making an interface that you can use for many purposes—from web page to CD-ROM interfaces to kiosk touch screens and more.

Setting Up the Interface

In this example, I'm using a slightly modified version of the brushed-metal texture that was described in Hour 16, "Special Effects"; see Figure 16.10. I'll also use the bevel technique that was used for several other examples in other chapters.

To follow along, open a new 600×600 image at 72 pixels per inch with the background color set to white and the image type set to 16.7 million colors. Then follow these steps:

1. Turn on the grid by choosing View, Grid.
2. Select the Selection tool (it's the small dashed-line rectangle icon).
3. In the Controls palette, set the Selection Type option to Rectangular and the Feather value to 10.
4. Draw a rectangular selection from 50, 50 to 550, 550. You can use the grid and the coordinates displayed at the lower-left of the screen to help you position the Selection tool.
5. Select the Flood Fill tool (it resembles a small, tipped-over paint bucket) and set the foreground color to black.
6. Click in the selection to fill it with black.
7. Save the selection by choosing Selections, Save as Alpha Channel.
8. Choose Selections, Select None.
9. Choose Image, Other, Emboss to add a bevel to the rectangle.
10. Choose Image, Mirror to have the bevel reversed (see Figure 20.9).

FIGURE 20.9.

Beveled rectangle.

11. Add a new layer and name it **Steel Plate**.
12. Load the saved selection by choosing Selections, Load from Alpha Channel.
13. Fill the selection with white.
14. Choose Image, Noise, Add.

20

15. Set %Noise to 100 and choose Random.

16. Choose Colors, Gray Scale to turn the noise into greyscale.

17. Choose Colors, Increase Color Depth, 16.7 million colors.

18. Choose Image, Blur, Motion Blur, set the Direction to 120, and set the Intensity to 25 pixels. This setting gives you the same brushed-metal look that was described in Hour 16.

19. To change the look a little, choose Image, Sharpen, Sharpen More. This modification brings out the texture of the metal a little more.

20. Make the Background layer active (you can do so by clicking on the layer's name in the Layers palette) and turn off the visibility of the Steel Plate layer. (To turn off a layer's visibility, simply click the Layer Visibility Toggle icon in the Layers palette.)

21. Select the Selection tool and set the Feather value to 0 in the Controls palette.

22. Select a rectangular area around the beveled rectangle.

23. Choose Selections, Invert.

24. Set the current background color to white and press Delete to fill the area around the beveled rectangle with white.

25. Make the Steel Plate layer visible again and set its blending mode to Overlay.

    You should have a nice beveled steel plate—perfect for the foundation of the interface (see Figure 20.10).

FIGURE 20.10.

Beveled steel plate.

26. If you've turned off the grid, as I have done, turn it back on by choosing View, Grid.

27. Add a new layer and name it **Indents**.

28. Using the grid as a guide, make a circular selection (set the Feather value to 1) that's about 60 pixels in radius in the upper-left corner of the image.

29. Fill the selection with a black-to-white linear blend at an angle of 120 degrees (see Figure 20.11).

FIGURE 20.11.

Indent added in upper-left corner.

30. Click-and-drag the Indent layer onto the Add New Layer icon at the lower-left of the Layers palette to duplicate it.

31. Use the Mover tool to move the indent on the new layer to the right corner of the plate.

32. Turn off the visibility of the Steel Plate and the Background layers.

33. Choose Layers, Merge, Merge Visible to merge the two indents onto one layer.

34. Click-and-drag this layer onto the Add New Layer icon to create another layer with the two indents on it.

35. Drag these indents to the bottom of the image (you might need to restore the visibility of the other layers to help you place the indents).

36. Turn off the visibility of the Steel Plate and Background layers again and merge the two Indents layers.

20

37. Rename the Indents layer **Indents**, as it has probably been renamed through all of this copying. You should now have three layers: the Background layer, the Steel Plate layer, and the Indents layer. Your image should resemble the one shown in Figure 20.12.

FIGURE 20.12.

Steel plate with indents in each corner.

38. Add another layer and name it **Screws**.

39. Select the Selection tool and, in the Controls palette, set the Type option to Circular and set the Feather value to 1.

40. Place the mouse pointer in the center of the upper-left indent (use the grid to help you place the pointer) and make a selection that's about 30 pixels in radius.

41. Set the foreground color to a light grey (I used R: 180, G: 180, B: 180) and the background color to a dark grey (I used R: 77, G: 77, B: 77).

42. Select the Flood Fill tool and, in the Controls palette, set the Fill Style to Sunburst Gradient.

43. Click the Options button and set the Vertical to 27 and the Horizontal to 30.

44. Click within the selected area to fill it with the gradient. This will be the screw's head.

45. Click-and-drag this layer onto the Add New Layer icon to duplicate the screw.

46. Drag the screw into place over the upper-right indent.

47. Turn off the visibility of all of the layers except the two layers with the screws.

48. Merge these two layers by choosing Layers, Merge, Merge Visible.

49. Drag the merged layer onto the Add New Layer icon to duplicate the layer.

50. Turn on the visibility of all of the layers so that you can position the bottom screws. Position the bottom screws over the bottom indents.

51. Turn off the visibility of all of the layers except the two that contain the screws.

52. Choose Layers, Merge, Merge Visible to merge the two Screws layers. Rename the layer **Screws**.

53. Turn on the visibility of all the layers. Your image should resemble the one shown in Figure 21.13.

FIGURE 20.13.

Steel plate with the indents and the screws in place.

Adding the Finishing Touches to the Interface

Now for the finishing touches. If you'd like, you can add a drop shadow (Image, Effects, Drop Shadow) to the screws.

I used the Drop Shadow effect to add a black shadow with the Opacity set to 70, the Blur set to 5, and both the Vertical and Horizontal Offsets set to 2. The drop shadow adds to the illusion that the interface is three-dimensional (see Figure 20.14).

You can leave the screws like this and call them rivets, or you can go ahead and add the slots. To add the slots, I use the same technique of creating one element and then copying its layer and moving the new element into place.

1. To create the first slot, add a new layer, call it **Slots,** and zoom in on the screw in the upper-left corner of the image.

2. Select the Selection tool and, in the Controls palette, set the Selection type to Rectangular, set the Feather value to 0, and turn off the Antialias option.

20

FIGURE 20.14.

Drop Shadow effect added to the screws.

3. Draw a rectangular selection over the screw head (see Figure 20.15).

FIGURE 20.15.

Making a rectangular selection for the slot in the screw head.

4. Swap the foreground and background colors by clicking the small, bent, two-headed arrow below the foreground/background color swatches.

5. Select the Flood Fill tool and, in the Controls palette, set the Fill Style to Linear Gradient.

6. Click the Options button to bring up the Flood Fill Options dialog box.

7. Set the Direction to 180 degrees and click OK.

8. Click in the rectangular selected area to fill it with the gradient.

9. Select the Deformations tool (it's the rectangular icon with dots at each corner and the center points of each side, top, and bottom) and use it to turn the slot 45 degrees (see Figure 20.16).

FIGURE 20.16.

The slot filled with a linear gradient and rotated 45 degrees.

10. Choose Selection, Select None.

11. Copy the Slots layer (drag-and-drop the layer onto the Add New Layer icon) and drag the second slot into place over the upper-right screw.

12. Merge these two layers by making all others invisible and choosing Layers, Merge, Merge Visible.

13. Drag the merged layer onto the Add New Layer icon and drag the second set of slots into place over the bottom screws.

14. Merge the two Slots layers and rename the layer **Slots**.

15. You should now have five separate layers: the Background, the Steel Plate, the Indents, the Screws, and the Slots.

16. You should probably lower the opacity of the Indents layer so that some of the steel plate shows through. You can adjust the opacity of any layer by making the layer active (click on the layer's name in the Layers palette) and moving the slider to the left. I set mine to about 60%.

Figure 20.17 shows my final image.

20

FIGURE 20.17.

The final steel plate and screws interface.

All that's left is to add some text, a logo, or some buttons. I discuss some of the methods for doing so in Hour 22, "Buttons and Seamless Tiles."

Summary

This was another fun hour. I've shown you how to create some neat effects that are not commonly done with Paint Shop Pro. I really hope that you'll see from these examples just how powerful Paint Shop Pro is and that you'll explore some ideas of your own.

In the next hour, I show you how to prepare your graphics for the web.

Workshop

The workshop contains a question and answer section to help answer the most commonly asked questions and quiz questions to help you solidify your understanding of the material covered.

Q&A

Q What other kinds of effects can be accomplished using the outline procedure described in this chapter?

A Outlining is a cool technique that has many uses. You could, for example, select many different objects at one time, using any number of selection techniques, and apply the effect to outline all the objects.

Q **What elements besides screws would be good to add to an interface?**

A Basically anything that adds to the illusion that you're after. You might, for example, add buttons, dials, animated dials, and more.

Q **How do you create the 3D look using gradients?**

A Because lighter objects appear to be closer than darker objects, gradients give objects a three-dimensional appearance. Going from light to dark, or vice versa, fools the eye into believing that a flat object has depth.

Quiz

1. Why do you have to use so many layers when outlining an irregularly shaped image or text?

2. Which tool do you use to add a texture or photo to text?

3. How does the Drop Shadow tool help you create a realistic-looking interface?

4. How do you merge two layers? Why would you want to do this?

Answers

1. You use the different layers to keep the objects separate and so that you can outline in one color and fill in another.

2. You can use several tools to achieve this effect. One way is to use the Paint Brushes tool and choose a texture from the Tool Controls tab in the Controls palette.

3. The drop shadow helps create depth in an image, giving a more realistic 3D quality to your images.

4. You can merge two or more layers by turning off all other layers' visibility and choosing Layers, Merge, Merge Visible. You would want to merge layers that won't need to be manipulated separately again to control the size of the file. The more layers an image has, the larger the file size.

20

PART V

Paint Shop Pro for the Web

Hour

Hour 21

Preparing Your Graphics for the Web

Today many digital artists are creating graphics for the World Wide Web. Creating images for the web, though, means working within certain limitations. You must be aware of things such as color palettes, dithering, anti-aliasing, and web file formats.

You must also be aware of file compression. You don't need to know about it at the same level as programmers do, but you must be aware of the difference it can make with your images. The following web-related issues are covered in this hour:

- Working with file formats
- Adjusting color depth
- Using palettes
- Previewing your images on the web
- Understanding hexadecimal notation
- Dithering and anti-aliasing

Working with File Formats

So what's the best way to compress your images? Currently, and unfortunately, only two file formats are available for web graphics. I say unfortunately not because of these two formats, but rather because of the lack of other choices. The current choices are GIF and JPG.

> Why compress your image files, anyway? Because compressing files saves disk space and because compressed files download faster from your web pages.

GIFs

GIF, for *Graphical Interchange Format*, is an image compression format originally developed by CompuServe. This format is one of the most popular formats for computer images. It also has a couple of features that make it appealing for web graphics. Like any other format, though, it also has some shortcomings. In addition to lacking some desirable features, the GIF format has recently been surrounded by copyright infringement problems. The mathematical algorithm used to compress the image information, called LZW (for Lempel-Ziv & Welch, the mathematicians who developed it), is patented by Unisys. (An *algorithm* is a mathematical formula that can be programmed in a computer language to perform a set of steps.)

Unisys has decided to charge developers licensing and royalty fees. This prospect didn't sit well with the Internet community at large. As a result, programmers on the web have banded together to create the PNG (pronounced "ping") format. This format is not currently supported on today's popular browsers. The situation should change shortly, though, with the Internet community pushing for PNG's inclusion. Despite this controversy, GIF has been and probably will continue to be around for a while.

GIFs: The Good, the Bad, and the Ugly

The GIF format, although somewhat limited, has some really good properties. For example, it can compress cartoons, illustrations, and images with large areas of similar color very well. Even with these types of images, though, the GIF format yields different results because of the way that the GIF compression algorithm works. You can see what I mean by looking at a couple of images (see Figures 21.1 and 21.2).

FIGURE 21.1.

Thick horizontal stripes: 1,292 bytes.

FIGURE 21.2.

Thick vertical stripes: 1,540 bytes.

Figures 21.1 and 21.2 are similar except that Figure 21.1 has horizontal bars and Figure 21.2 has vertical bars. Aside from that, they are both the same size and have the same number of colors. Note the file sizes, though. Figure 21.2 is 248 bytes bigger than Figure 21.1. That's almost 20% bigger. Take a look at a few more images (Figures 21.3 and 21.4), and then you can examine why this size difference occurs.

FIGURE 21.3.

Thin horizontal stripes: 1,299 bytes.

FIGURE 21.4.

Thin vertical stripes: 2,679 bytes.

Wow! There's an even bigger difference between the file size of Figure 21.3 and that of Figure 21.4. The difference is 1,380 bytes—a whopping 106%. What's interesting, as well, is that there is only a very small difference in file size between Figure 21.1 and Figure 21.3—only seven bytes.

21

The way that GIF format compresses information explains the difference in file size. Large blocks of identical information that read from the top left and go across toward the right are well compressed. On the other hand, when information changes (for example, a color change), the GIF compression method starts to lose its power.

A GIF image in one solid color the same size as Figures 21.1 through 21.4 is 1,146 bytes—not much smaller than Figures 21.1 and 21.3. You can see the losses that happen, though, when you start breaking up the horizontal runs of a single color. Imagine how much room a vertical gradient would take up!

What all of this means to you as a web graphic designer is that there are no hard-and-fast rules when it comes to image compression. Sometimes GIF will be the method of choice, and sometimes it won't be. You'll really have to examine each image independently. For the most part, though, GIF works well with images that have a limited color palette.

There are also some cases when the only choice is to use the GIF format. One of these is when you want some of the image's information to be transparent.

Transparent GIFs

Transparent GIFs are handy when you have a background pattern on your web pages. Without the transparency option, you're limited to having a rectangle around your images, as in Figure 21.5.

FIGURE 21.5.

Example of nontransparent GIF.

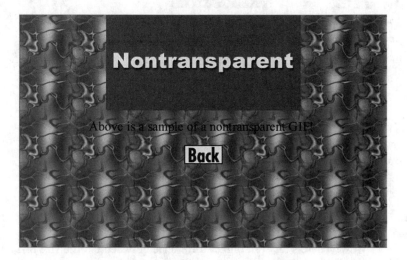

Figure 21.5 shows a web page with a GIF at the top. The GIF wasn't saved with the transparency option activated. As a result, a dark rectangle appears around the word *Nontransparent*. Figure 21.6 shows the same web page; in this example, however, the GIF was saved with the transparency option turned on.

FIGURE 21.6.

Example of transparent GIF.

Notice how the background pattern is visible around, and even between, the letters. This transparency option is available in most of today's graphics programs.

Saving Transparent GIFs with Paint Shop Pro

To use Paint Shop Pro to save a transparent GIF, follow these steps:

1. Open a new image (or an existing one if you'd like to remove its background).
2. Create the image you want. I'm using the stylized ampersand shown in Figure 21.7.

FIGURE 21.7.

Stylized ampersand.

21

Before you can activate the transparency option, however, you must make the following changes:

3. Decrease the color resolution to 256 or less. Choose Colors, Decrease Color Depth, 256-Colors (8-bit). If you have more than one layer, you'll be warned that you must flatten the image first. You can do so by clicking Yes in the warning message box.

> You might want to make sure that you've saved a copy of your file in the native Paint Shop Pro format before you reduce the colors and save the file as a GIF. This way you'll have the original file with its layers and channels intact should you need to make changes in the future.

4. Set the options you want to use in the Decrease Color Depth dialog box and click OK.

5. Set the current background color to the color you want to become transparent. You can set the current background color by clicking on the background color swatch and choosing a color from the color picker. Alternatively, you can select the Dropper tool and right-click on the image on the color you want to set the background color to. This method is a great way to select the transparent color.

6. Choose Colors, Set Palette Transparency. In the dialog box that appears, select Set the Transparency Value to the Current Background Color and click OK. You can choose to set the transparent color to No Transparency (which would mean having no transparent color) or to a specific palette entry.

7. You can, in this version, even preview the transparency. Choose Colors, View Palette Transparency (see Figure 21.8).

FIGURE 21.8.

Stylized ampersand as a transparent GIF.

All that's left is to save your image as a GIF. To do so, choose File, Save As and then choose GIF from the Save As Type pull-down menu. To make sure that the transparency works properly, click on the Options button and make sure that the Version is set to version 89a.

JPGs

JPGs or, more properly, JPEGs, for *Joint Photographic Experts Group* (pronounced "jay-pegs") is a somewhat misunderstood compression method. Images compressed using the JPG algorithm often get a bad rap from users who view the resulting images with 256-color systems. Because JPGs are 24-bit images, they often dither badly on 8-bit systems. On a 16- or 24-bit system, however, a JPG saved with a high-quality setting can be a fairly high-quality image. In addition, the JPG image is often much smaller than the same image saved with another compression method.

Did You Lose Something?

Another misunderstood aspect of JPG files is that the compression algorithm used is known as a *lossy compression method*. In other words, some information is discarded during compression. Losing information may seem like a problem but, in fact, it saves a lot of space while changing the quality very little. With an appropriate quality setting, the lost information is not readily visible to the human eye. The savings and the quality work against each other, though, as you can see from Figures 21.9 through 21.11. These figures were saved with Ulead's SmartSaver from within Paint Shop Pro 5.

SmartSaver is an export plug-in available from Ulead. This plug-in enables you to export GIFs, JPGs, and PNGs from within Paint Shop Pro. SmartSaver offers real-time previews, varying levels of compression, color depth, and more.

Figure 21.9 was saved at 100% quality and is 82,098 bytes. It closely resembles the original scan, which is 449,974 bytes.

FIGURE 21.9.

Scan of Marianne saved as 100% quality JPG.

21

Figure 21.10 was saved in the same manner except that the setting was changed to 55%. I'm not sure what the final print will look like in the book, but on my screen it was very difficult to see any difference. This version, though, takes up only 9,443 bytes. Quite a large savings.

FIGURE 21.10.

Scan of Marianne saved as 55% quality JPG.

The final JPG (Figure 21.11) was saved with a setting of 10% quality. Although this image compressed the best, I think you'll agree that the last little saving in disk space (and download time) wasn't worth it. This file, which now takes up 3,593 bytes, isn't the best quality.

FIGURE 21.11.

Scan of Marianne saved as 10% quality JPG.

You can see, though, that the JPG format enables you to save a lot of space and bandwidth without compromising the quality of your web graphics. Another problem that can occur because of the lossy compression method happens to images that are edited and resaved in the JPG format. Figure 21.12 is a 300% blowup of the GrafX Design logo. Figure 21.13 shows the same logo edited and resaved as a JPG five times.

FIGURE 21.12.

GrafX Design logo saved as a JPG.

FIGURE 21.13.

GrafX Design logo edited and resaved as a JPG five times.

Notice the marks around the image in Figure 21.13. They're in Figure 21.12, as well, but they're not as noticeable. These marks are called *artifacts* and are a result of the way that the JPG compression algorithm works. Along with the added artifacts, resaving a JPG many times can actually add to the size of the final image.

The solution? Always save your images in a 24-bit *lossless format* such as BMP, PCX, or TIFF.

Lossless compression formats use a method of compression that assures that no information is lost. An image can be compressed and uncompressed many times with no changes to the image. Compared to lossless compression formats, lossy compression methods achieve much higher compression ratios, but they do so by discarding some of the information that makes up the image. Normally, the fact that these methods discard information is not a problem. The compression algorithms discard information in such a way that the changes are too subtle to be picked up by the human eye. The changes can become apparent, though, at very high compression rates or after successive compressions.

21

An even better approach is to save your work in the format of the image program you're using. For example, you should always save a copy of any important graphic being worked on in Paint Shop Pro as a PSP file. Keeping these extra copies enables you to save the program's extra features along with your images. Saving a PSP file in Paint Shop Pro, for example, keeps all the layer and channel information. Most of the larger imaging programs have their own formats. These programs normally have the option of saving both GIF and JPG web-ready images, as well.

Why Use JPG?

After reading the last bit about JPGs and how this method discards some information, you may be wondering why you should use this format for your web graphics. Take another look at Figures 21.9 and 21.10. Figure 21.9 is more than 82,000 bytes, and Figure 21.10 is just over 9,000 bytes! I doubt that you can really tell the difference between the two. I normally save with a much higher setting and was rather surprised myself at the quality of Figure 21.10.

Remember, too, that Figure 21.9 is a JPG that is already much smaller than the original 24-bit image. The bottom line is if you have an image with a subtle blend of color, such as a portrait or a gradient, JPG is a good format.

GIF or JPG?

The debate over which format is better still rages every so often on Usenet. My opinion is that both formats have their place just as the native formats of the various image programs do. Under some circumstances, a JPG beats out a GIF file in terms of quality and size; at other times the best choice is GIF. Personally, I take the time to view my images in both formats using SmartSaver. I also take the time to play around with the number of colors when previewing my images as GIFs, as well as trying out the different palettes.

When I'm previewing a JPG, I try different quality settings. There really is no hard-and-fast answer. Even after creating more computer graphics than I can count, I still play around with each new image to get the best quality/size ratio that I can.

Adjusting Color Depth

Color depth is a way of describing how many colors your hardware and software are capable of displaying. The buzzwords most often used are 8-bit, 16-bit, and 24-bit. Of course, color depth is sometimes described by the actual number of colors being displayed, such as 256 colors or 16.7 million colors.

Hardware is the real determining factor. Your web browser, for example, will display as many colors as your system can use. The next limiting factor is the type of image being displayed. GIFs are capable of displaying only 256 separate colors. These colors can, however, be chosen from all 16.7 million available colors. JPGs can display up to 16.7 million colors, which makes the JPG format a popular choice for photographs and other real-world images.

8-Bit Color

Eight-bit or 256 colors is what many systems use, although they are often capable of displaying more. Sometimes referred to as Video Gate Array (VGA), 8-bit is somewhat limited. With your system set to 8-bit, you're at the mercy of your browser software, as you'll see later in the section on palettes.

16-Bit Color

Sixteen-bit color, often referred to as "hi color," is a good choice if your system's video memory is limited. Using 16-bit color is a great compromise between speed and color. With 16-bit color, up to 64,000 colors are possible (65,536 actually). With 64,000 colors, your web viewing experience will be much more enriched. Using this color depth reduces the need for dithering.

Dithering, a process used to fool the eye into seeing more colors than are actually available, is discussed in depth a little later in this hour.

24-Bit Color

Twenty-four–bit is the best color depth to use when creating and viewing computer images. To use this color depth, though, your video card must have at least 1MB of memory. The reason is that for each pixel you must have 24-bits (or 3 bytes) of memory available. With a little simple arithmetic, you can see that a 640×480 screen, which means 307,200 (640×480) pixels, requires 307,200×3 bytes (or 307,200 pixels×3 bytes per pixel), which equals 921,600 bytes. Now that you have a basic understanding of color depth, it's time to look at palettes.

Using Palettes

Traditionally, a palette was a surface on which an artist would mix the colors before applying them to the canvas. In computer graphics, a palette is somewhat similar. Most graphics programs have a window where you can pick your colors. In certain circumstances, your color choices are limited. Those limited sets of colors are also referred to as *palettes*.

21

Palettes are more important when working with GIF images. Because of their limited color depth, GIF images can use only a select palette. This palette, though, can contain a different selection of colors. Sometimes you have control over the selection of the colors and, unfortunately, sometimes you don't.

Problems with Limited Palettes

One problem associated with limited palettes is that if you choose to work with a limited palette while creating your images, many of the features of your graphics programs will not be available to you. Options such as drop shadows and blurring need to have access to the full range of colors to do their magic. The alternative here is to create your image using the higher color depth and then reduce the depth.

> You should always keep a copy of the image with its color depth set at the higher resolution. This extra copy makes applying subsequent changes much easier. Saving your image as a BMP, a TIF, or a PCX, for example, is something you should always consider doing. These formats tend to take up a little more room, though, so you might also want to consider having some sort of backup system if you're going to be creating lots of images.

How to Build or Select a Palette

You can build a palette in a number of ways. You can load an indexed (or GIF) image into your graphics program. Having done so, the palette associated with that image will be available to you. Most software also allows you to build a palette color by color. You can open up the palette and add, edit, or remove colors from it. Figure 21.14 shows the Edit Palette dialog box from Paint Shop Pro.

FIGURE 21.14.

The Edit Palette dialog box.

Double-clicking on one of the colors in the Edit Palette dialog box brings up the Color dialog box (see Figure 21.15).

FIGURE 21.15.

The Color dialog box.

You can change the color you double-clicked to any one of 16.7 million other colors. In Paint Shop Pro, just enter the RGB values in the boxes in the lower-left corner of the dialog box. This new color is then available in the palette. Note that the HSL model is available in the Color dialog box, as well.

Exact Palette

The *exact palette* is built from the colors currently being used in an image. If the number of colors exceeds that for the palette you're building, you can change some of the colors to others that are similar or you can allow the program to dither the colors for you. Normally, this becomes an issue only when you need to convert the image to a lower color resolution mode before saving the image.

Adaptive Palette

Most web browsers use an *adaptive palette* when loading an image that doesn't fit their own color palette. There are a few gotchas involved here, though. You'll be okay if all the images share the same palette. If, on the other hand, you have a couple of images that use different palettes, you may find that your images have dithered terribly.

The problem is that while you're working on your images, you're probably working on them one at a time, right? So you create one image, save it, and go on to create the next one. You get this great idea for a different set of colors and create the second image with a completely new color scheme from the first. You then save the image after adjusting the mode appropriately. Still no problem.

21

You then sign on to the Internet and load your web page. Oh oh! The colors on both images look really bad. What happened? Well, what happened is that if the browser is running on an 8-bit setup, it can't show you the 256 colors from one image and another 256 from the next. It can, after all, display only 256 different colors at one time. This limitation brings us to the dreaded Netscape or web palette, discussed next.

Web Palette

The web palette is the scourge of web graphics artists the world over. This palette consists of 216 colors that, if used when constructing your images, display your images the same way on every platform.

I say scourge because 216 colors is not very many, and the color choices are abysmal. For example, there are only 6 shades of grey.

 You can download the web palette from Jasc Software Inc.'s site at http://www.jasc.com or at GrafX Design's web site at http://www.grafx-design.com.

Why 216 colors and not 256? Because the operating system, Windows, for example, and the browser, Netscape, let's say, use up 40 colors between them, which leaves 216 colors. This palette is sometimes called *the cube*, which refers to its being a 6×6×6 (6 times 6 times 6 equals 216) cube: six colors wide, six colors high, and six sides.

Because of the popularity of web graphics, many graphics programs now include a version of the web palette. Although this feature makes the process of creating images that use this set of colors easier, it doesn't change the fact that you are limited to this particular color set.

So, what can you do? One answer is to use your own set of colors, being careful that all your images use the same restricted palette. The other option is to hope that many readers of your pages will be using machines capable of displaying more than 256 colors. I wouldn't bet on this case for a little while, though. Many web surfers are still using older 386 machines.

Of course, you could build your graphics with these limitations in mind and take them into account when the images are really important for navigation around your site.

Previewing Your Images in SmartSaver

One product that can help if you're using a high-color resolution system and are worried about what your readers will see is Ulead's SmartSaver software (see Figure 21.16).

FIGURE 21.16.

Ulead's SmartSaver.

Although you are seeing the preview in black and white, you can probably tell that there's not much difference between the image on the left, the original, and the image on the right. The image on the right is what my GrafX Design logo would look like when displayed using the Netscape palette. Even though I eventually saved this image as a JPG to take advantage of the subtler gradient available when using a higher-color resolution, I was pretty sure that the readers who ventured onto my pages wouldn't be too disappointed by the quality of this image. To add some assurance, I created most of the subsequent images with a color palette that was close to the chrome-and-blue scheme I had used for the main logo.

SmartSaver is valuable for more than its preview screen, though. This software also enables you to choose from a wider range of colors than would normally be available. Notice the Colors spin control near the bottom left of Figure 21.16. You can set any value between 16 and 216. Playing with the numbers means that you can shave some extra weight off your images while keeping the colors and quality at an acceptable level.

SmartSaver works with both GIF and JPG images and lets you set a variable quality for JPGs, as well. SmartSaver acts as a "File, Export" extension to Paint Shop Pro. You can also use SmartSaver on a standalone basis. Either way, SmartSaver is something to consider if you create a lot of web graphics.

SmartSaver is a shareware product available from Ulead. Registration is about $29. You can download a trial version from Ulead's web site at `http://www.ulead.com`. Although SmartSaver doesn't overcome the web palette limitations, it reduces the frustration level.

21

Understanding Dithering

Dithering, which applies only to GIF images, is one of those big bugaboos that is constantly argued about on Usenet. *Dithering,* put simply, is a process of constructing one color from a combination of other colors. You may remember from school how blue and yellow, when mixed together, give you green. Color mixing is the principle behind dithering.

In practice, dithering is quite complex. There are several mathematical functions available when dithering images. One of these is known as *diffusion* (see Figure 21.19). The dithering processes available with your software depends on which program you're using. Just as you must decide which format to save your files in, you must also select which dithering process to use. I suggest experimenting with several images to see which method best suits a particular image. The dithering choice is usually made when you decrease the color depth of an image.

Image software, be it your graphics program or your browser, resorts to dithering when it cannot display the entire color palette of an image. The results can vary. Figure 21.17 is an image that hasn't had its color reduced.

FIGURE 21.17.

Twenty-four–bit image.

Figure 21.18 is the same image reduced to 16 colors (or 16 levels of grey, if you will). No dithering has been applied.

FIGURE 21.18.

Sixteen-color image with no dithering.

Notice the distinct banding in Figure 21.18. Without the help of dithering, the process to reduce the number of colors must choose a nearest match. On the other hand, the diffusion method of dithering was applied to Figure 21.19 during color reduction.

FIGURE 21.19.

Sixteen-color image reduced with diffusion dithering.

Some people may regard the speckling, which is a result of the dithering, as unacceptable. You'll have to decide how to handle this problem when it comes to designing your own web graphics. If you're going to display 256-color images that were created as 24-bit images, you'll have to decide whether to dither. One option is to choose colors that closely match those available in the palette that the images will ultimately be displayed with.

Understanding Anti-Aliasing

Before I explain what anti-aliasing is, I'll cover aliasing. These two subjects are, of course, closely related. People almost never discuss aliasing, though.

Aliasing

Aliasing is what happens when analog data is represented on a digital system. A curved line drawn on a grid is a good example of analog data on a digital system (see Figure 21.20).

FIGURE 21.20.

Line of grid representing analog data on digital system.

When the analog data is converted to digital, some problems arise. The digital system in this example is the grid. To convert the analog line to a digital line, each point in the grid may either represent a point in the line, by being filled in, or represent an area where the line does not exist, by remaining white. A square cannot be partly filled; it must be either filled in or not. That's all part of its being digital.

21

Okay no problem, right? The line goes through the different squares, so you fill in each square that the line goes through. This requirement isn't a problem with some portions of the line, for example, the portion circled in Figure 21.21.

FIGURE 21.21.

A portion of the line easily converted to digital.

But what about sections like the one circled in Figure 21.22?

FIGURE 21.22.

Portion of line not easily converted to digital.

That portion cuts right across the intersection between four points. That's where aliasing comes in. An algorithm decides where all the portions fit in the digital system.

Figure 21.23 demonstrates what the resulting digital line might look like.

See how it looks choppy. The same thing will happen to, for example, any aliased text you display on your web pages.

Anti-Aliasing

Is there a solution? Yep! It comes in the form of, ta-da, *anti-aliasing*. What anti-aliasing attempts to do, using mathematics again, is to fill in some of the digital system with colors that are between the two adjoining colors. In this case, a medium grey would be between the black and the white. Some grey squares placed in the grid might help soften up the *jaggies* (see Figure 21.24).

FIGURE 21.23.

Digital version of line.

FIGURE 21.24.

Anti-aliased line.

(Keep in mind that this example was hand drawn and that the resolution of the final printing in the book may not show an improvement.)

To give you a better idea of aliased versus anti-aliased, then, here are a couple of lines drawn with Paint Shop Pro. The first, Figure 21.25, is aliased.

FIGURE 21.25.

Aliased line.

Figure 21.26 is an anti-aliased line drawn in Paint Shop Pro.

So there'll be no mistaking the difference, Figures 21.27 and 21.28 are the aliased and the anti-aliased lines blown up 500%.

21

FIGURE 21.26.

Anti-aliased line.

FIGURE 21.27.

Aliased line at 500%.

FIGURE 21.28.

Anti-aliased line at 500%.

Notice the jagged appearance of the line in Figure 21.27, whereas the line in Figure 21.28 is smooth. Of course, at this resolution, the line in Figure 21.28 seems a little blurry. This factor is something else to consider when using the anti-aliasing option for your graphics. The fuzziness can be especially problematic with text. Text, as well as the rest of an image, is generally anti-aliased whenever it is resized, so you may want to add text only after you have decided on the final size of your image. This technique helps keep your text more readable.

Summary

Hour 21 was another fun hour. There was a lot of information here, though, and I covered a lot of theory. You are now well armed when it comes to creating web graphics. Hour 22, "Buttons and Seamless Tiles," covers creating buttons, GIFs, and other images that you can use on your web pages.

Workshop

The workshop contains a question and answer section to help answer the most commonly asked questions and quiz questions to help you solidify your understanding of the material covered.

Q&A

Q What is an algorithm?

A An *algorithm* describes a set of steps designed to solve a particular problem. The algorithm can even start out as a mathematical expression that programmers convert into a programming language so that a computer can solve the problem.

Q How do you pronounce GIF?

A Believe it or not, this question appears, from time to time, on Usenet. When it does, it sparks a huge debate that often goes on for weeks at a time. It can be pronounced either with a soft *G,* as in *JIF,* or with a hard *G,* as in *GIFT.* I've held discussions with someone who uses the former, while I happily go on using the latter. Because we both understood what we were discussing, it didn't really matter. Of course, as evidenced by the heated Usenet debates, some people like to make an issue out of it. And so goes Usenet.

Q What is bandwidth?

A *Bandwidth* describes how much information can travel over a system such as the Internet. Although tons of data can travel very quickly over fiber-optic cables, few of us have this state-of-the-art cabling coming into our homes or offices. The bandwidth of the copper wiring that the phone system uses, which most of us connect to the web with, is somewhat limited. Therefore, keeping file sizes down is important. Of course, you don't want to lose too much image quality, so there's a constant battle between bandwidth and image integrity.

21

Q Where does the number 65,526 colors come from in 16-bit color?

A The number 65,536 is the number you'd get if you raised 2 to the power of 16 (16-bits, bits equalling two possibilities: on and off or 0 and 1). Likewise, 2 raised to the power of 8 yields 256—256 colors equal 8 bits. Finally, 24-bit equals 2 raised to the power of 24 (which equals 16.7 million colors).

Q What if I have an 8-bit system? What do I do about using 24-bit mode when creating my images?

A Although the program will be set internally to 24-bit, you'll still see only 8-bit images on your screen. As long as the software is set to high-color resolution, there should be no problem. Even though your hardware may be limited to 8-bit color, you'll have to set the software to the higher-color resolution to work with all the possible options.

Quiz

1. Which two file formats can you currently use for web graphics, and why only these two?

2. What is a transparent GIF? What does it help you do?

3. What is dithering?

4. How does anti-aliasing improve the quality of your images?

Answers

1. You can currently use the GIF and JPG file formats when saving your images for the web. These two formats are the only formats that today's web browsers recognize.

2. A transparent GIF is an image saved in the GIF format with one particular color tagged so that the software displaying the GIF image will not display that one tagged color, allowing whatever is behind this portion of the image to show through. This feature enables you to create images that can have irregular edges instead of being surrounded by a rectangle.

3. Dithering is a way of decreasing the color depth of an image. The decrease in color depth is performed in such a way that subtle changes in the original are "faked" through the use of patterns using fewer colors.

4. Anti-aliasing improves the look of an image by softening the edges. Anti-aliasing is accomplished by adding pixels using colors that lie between the two colors that make up the edges.

HOUR 22

Buttons and Seamless Tiles

When it comes to web sites, you'll need to create several types of graphics. The most common types are buttons and seamless tiles. Fortunately, Paint Shop Pro excels at helping you create these types of graphics.

The following techniques related to buttons and tiles are covered in this hour:

- Creating ordinary buttons
- Creating 3D textured buttons
- Creating seamless tiles
- Creating seamless tiles with Paint Shop Pro

Creating Buttons

Buttons are an important part of any web page. They help your visitors navigate through your site and can even tell people a little about your style and the style of your site.

Buttons can range from the plain and ordinary, such as regular filled rectangles, to the more elaborate, such as 3D buttons, to the outrageous, such as wildly textured and weirdly shaped buttons.

Ordinary Buttons

You can create simple buttons with ease in Paint Shop Pro. Simply select the Shapes tool (it resembles an outlined square), set the foreground color to the color you want your buttons to be, and draw some shapes.

You'll want to add text, of course, or some type of icon (see Figure 22.1).

FIGURE 22.1.

Some simple buttons created in Paint Shop Pro.

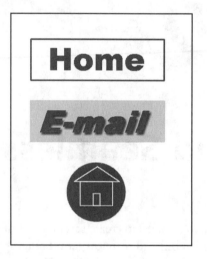

The buttons shown in Figure 22.1 were created with techniques from the early hours in this book. To create these images, I used tools such as the Shapes tool, the Text tool, and the Line tool.

Simple buttons are okay and, in some cases, are even better than something more elaborate. If you're selling a product, for example, that has nothing to do with graphics and/or imaging, you might not want the navigational elements on your site to get in the way of the product you're actually selling.

If, however, you want something a little flashier, you're in luck. Paint Shop Pro does that, too, with a little help from you, the digital artist.

More Elaborate Buttons

You can get more elaborate by simply adding shadows, or adding some dimensionality, to your buttons. To get the effect of depth, you'll need to make a few selections and use

22

some gradients. Here's how you can add depth to a rectangular button that would ordinarily be, well… ordinary:

1. Open a new image at the size you want your button to be (or a little larger).

2. Select the Selection tool (it resembles a dashed-line rectangle) and, in the Controls palette, set the selection type to Rectangle.

3. Draw a rectangular selection that mostly fills the image.

4. Set the foreground color to a light shade of the color you want the button to be and set the background color to a dark shade of the color you want the button to be. I chose light blue and dark blue.

5. Select the Flood Fill tool (it resembles a tipped-over paint bucket) and, in the Controls palette, set the fill style to linear gradient.

6. Click the Options button and set the Direction to 135 degrees.

7. Click OK.

8. Click within the selection to fill the area with the gradient (see Figure 22.2).

FIGURE 22.2.

The beginnings of a 3D rectangular button.

9. Choose Selections, Modify, Contract and enter a number that will give you the size of border that you want. Try 10 or so, depending on the size of your button.

10. Swap the foreground and background colors by clicking on the small, bent, two-headed arrow below the foreground/background color swatches.

11. In the Controls palette, set the Match mode to none. This setting ensures that the complete selection is filled, even though it is currently filled with a gradient. Normally, you'll want the fill to stop when it "sees" a color change. Choosing none for the Match mode makes the fill cover everything, regardless of what's currently occupying the space.

12. Click within the selected area to fill the inner rectangle with the opposite linear gradient (see Figure 22.3).

These buttons are easy to make, can be made with virtually any shape, and look great on a web page. They are also easy to modify for any color scheme.

FIGURE 22.3.

A completed 3D rec-
tangular button.

Complex 3D Textured Buttons

Paint Shop Pro also enables you to create textured 3D buttons. The next exercise shows you how to use layers and blending modes, along with selections, to create more-complex buttons.

Open a new file and give it 200 as the width and 100 as the height. Also, make sure you use 16.7 million as the color depth. Set the background color of the image to white for now. Then follow these steps:

1. Create a new layer by clicking on the Add New Layer icon in the lower-left corner of the Layers palette.

2. Select the Selection tool and, under the Tool Controls tab in the Controls palette, set the selection type to Rectangle and set Feather to 0.

3. Draw a rectangular selection as shown in Figure 22.4.

FIGURE 22.4.

A rectangular
selection.

4. Select the Flood Fill tool and fill the selection with black. You can do so by setting the foreground color to black, selecting the Flood Fill tool, setting the Fill Style to Solid Color in the Tool Controls, and clicking within the rectangular selected area. You'll now have a black rectangle.

5. Select the Selection tool and set the style to Ellipse, set Feather to 0, and turn off the Antialias option.

6. Place the cursor's crosshairs in the middle of the left side of the black rectangle and draw down and to the left until you have an ellipse that covers part of the left side of the rectangle (see Figure 22.5).

FIGURE 22.5.

An elliptical selection drawn on the left side of the rectangle.

22

7. Set the Protect Transparency toggle to on (it's the second icon to the right of the layer name in the Layers palette, and it resembles a small lock). The small green lock next to the layer's name should turn red.

8. Set the foreground color to a shade of grey, select the Flood Fill tool, set the Fill Style to Solid Color, and click in the selected area. Only that part of the area taken up by the button should turn grey (see Figure 22.6).

FIGURE 22.6.

An elliptical selection partially filled with grey.

9. Select the Mover tool, right-click on the elliptical selection, and drag it to the right side of the black rectangle. Select the Flood Fill tool and fill the right ellipse with the same grey color (see Figure 22.7).

FIGURE 22.7.

Both ellipses filled with grey.

10. Select the Selection tool, set the selection type to Rectangle, and turn off anti-aliasing. Make a rectangular selection that covers about the top third of the button. Set the foreground color to black and the background color to white. Select the Flood Fill tool, set the Fill Style to Linear Gradient, the Match mode to RGB, the Tolerance to 0, the Opacity to 100%, and click the Options button.

11. Set the Angle to 180 and click OK.

12. Click anywhere in the black area within the selection.

13. Select the Selection tool and position the cursor just at the bottom of the current selection. Make a new selection that covers the bottom two-thirds of the button.

14. Swap the foreground/background colors by clicking on the small bent two-headed arrow at the lower left of the foreground/background color swatches.

15. Select the Flood Fill tool and click somewhere on the remaining black area. You should have something that resembles Figure 22.8.

FIGURE 22.8.

Two gradients fill the middle of the button.

16. Choose Selections, Select None.

17. Select the Dropper tool and pick up a light color from the gradient. Get close to the highlight, but don't take the actual highlight color.

18. Select the Flood Fill tool, set the Fill Style to Solid Color, and click on the left side of the button to fill it with a much lighter grey.

19. Select the Dropper tool and pick up a color from the shadowed area of the button. Use the Flood Fill tool to fill the right side of the button with the darker grey color.

20. Select the Magic Wand tool (it resembles a small magic wand) and click outside of the button. Choose Selections, Invert to invert the selection. This technique is a great way to select an area that has several colors.

21. Choose Image, Blur, Gaussian Blur and set the value to about 2.00.

You'll now have a great 3D button, as shown in Figure 22.9.

FIGURE 22.9.

3D button created with selections, fills, and a Gaussian Blur.

Let's see what else you can do using the Layers feature, though. Try these steps:

1. Open a textured file. You can find textured images all over the web, or you can invent your own. This book shows you how to create a wood texture (Hour 10, "Creating Cool Text Effects") and a brushed-metal texture (Hour 16, "Special Effects").

2. To keep the same size selection, choose Edit, Copy with the first image (the button) as current. Make the texture file current and choose Edit, Paste, As New Layer.

3. Choose the Mover tool and move the button around until it covers that area of the texture that you'd like to copy. Choose the Magic Wand tool and click somewhere outside the button. Choose Selections, Invert. Make the texture layer current and choose Edit, Copy.

4. Make the button image current. Choose Selections, None and choose Edit, Paste, As New Layer. If you need to move the texture around so that it covers the button, you can use the Mover tool.

5. With the texture in place, set the Texture layer's mode to Overlay. (The Layer Blending mode can be set from the pull-down menu in the Layers palette; see Figure 22.10.)

FIGURE 22.10.

Texture overlaid on 3D button.

If you find, like I do, that the button is a little too bright or that there should be more texture showing, no problem. Obviously, you can't add to the opacity of the texture—it's at the max. However, you can reduce the opacity of the Button layer. Try setting it to about 70%. Hmmm... That doesn't seem to have any effect. Try turning off the Background layer. Voilà!!! A more professional button would be hard to find (see Figure 22.11).

FIGURE 22.11.

Final 3D, textured button.

Creating Seamless Tiles

A *seamless tile* is an image that, when tiled or repeated, forms a seamless pattern. Therefore, you can use a relatively small image file that will tile itself on your web page. Creating seamless tiles is something that is discussed constantly on Usenet.

The object, of course, is to get the sides to match up so that the smaller tile appears to be one large image when it's placed on your pages.

Before going on to show you how to create a seamless tile, I'll explain the basic principles.

The Basics of Seamless Tiles

The object of a seamless tile, once again, is to get the edges of your image to match up so that when the image is tiled, it appears to be one big image. Demonstrating this is easier, by far, than trying to explain it.

Suppose you have an image that you want to tile and suppose the image is square. (This technique works just as well if the image is a rectangle.) The goal is to swap the diagonal quarters of the image. (I told you this concept was hard to explain.) To get a better idea of what I'm talking about, take a look at the diagram in Figure 22.12.

FIGURE 22.12.

Quartered image showing original placement of quarters.

What you need to do is cut the image into quarters and swap the diagonal corners. This step allows your image to tile seamlessly. When you move the pieces, the image should resemble Figure 22.13.

FIGURE 22.13.

Quartered image with final placement of quarters.

The reason this technique works is hard to see, but essentially you're cutting the image and rearranging it so that the edges formed by the cutting process are on the outside of the new image. Because the new edges were joined before you cut them, they match up when the image is tiled. Although this process is hard to visualize, it does work.

Figure 22.14 shows a textured image created with Kai's Power Tool Texture Explorer.

FIGURE 22.14.

Textured image created with Kai's Power Tools.

Figure 22.15 shows the same image with the corners numbered as in Figure 22.12.

FIGURE 22.15.

Textured image showing numbered quarters.

Of course, you don't have to draw the numbers in over the image. I've done so here to demonstrate the process more clearly. Figure 22.16 is the image after the quarters have been swapped. Note that the numbers are still in place.

FIGURE 22.16.

Textured image showing numbered quarters with corners swapped for tiling.

Figure 22.17 is the image with the quarters swapped and the numbers removed. This image will now tile seamlessly.

You may notice, however, that although the edges now match up, the center of the image has a vertical and a horizontal seam running through it.

22

FIGURE 22.17.

Textured image with quarters swapped for tiling.

If you get rid of the vertical and horizontal seams, this image will be ready to tile. The way to get rid of the seam is to use the Clone tool. Although it's a little difficult to master, the tool is very effective, as you'll see in the next section.

Creating Seamless Tiles with Paint Shop Pro

Creating seamless tiles with Paint Shop Pro requires a little work; you must cut and paste the four quarters yourself. Follow these steps to create your own tiles:

1. Open a textured image and note its dimensions. This information is visible on the status bar at the bottom right of the screen.

2. Create a new file with the same dimensions as the textured image (see Figure 22.18).

FIGURE 22.18.

Textured image and new image in Paint Shop Pro.

As described earlier in this hour, you must swap the diagonally opposed quarters.

3. Select the Selection tool and set its selection type to Rectangle and Feather to 0.

4. Place the cursor in the middle of the textured image. Remember that computers start counting at zero, not one. Therefore, the middle of the sample 200×200 textured file will be 99, 99 not 100, 100. You can see where you are on the image by looking at the mouse coordinates displayed at the bottom left of the Paint Shop Pro screen.

5. With the cursor in the middle of the image, click-and-drag the mouse to the upper-left corner of the image. Release the mouse and choose Edit, Copy.

6. Click somewhere in the new image to make it current and choose Edit, Paste, As New Selection.

7. Move the selection into the opposite corner of the new image from where it was in the textured image (see Figure 22.19).

22

FIGURE 22.19.

First corner moved to new image.

8. Continue cutting and pasting until all quarters have been moved to the new file (see Figure 22.20).

FIGURE 22.20.

All quarters moved to new image.

9. Select the Clone Brush tool (it resembles two small brushes) and right-click to select a source area. Move the mouse around the seamed center area, drawing over the seams until you can no longer distinguish the seams.

You can also use the Paint Brushes tool to fine-tune the image. After using the Clone Brush tool and working with it a bit, I ended up with the image in Figure 22.21.

FIGURE 22.21.

Final seamless tile in Paint Shop Pro.

To see what the final seamless background would look like, I created a new 600×600 image in Paint Shop Pro and, using the Paint Bucket tool, filled the new image with the seamless tile (see Figure 22.22).

FIGURE 22.22.

Tiled example of final seamless tile.

Summary

You can find tutorials and techniques for creating more types of web graphics all over the web. You might want to start at GrafX Design (`http://www.grafx-design.com`) or at Jasc Software Inc. (`http://www.jasc.com`).

That's pretty much it for the part of the book that covers Paint Shop Pro. The next two hours show you how to use Animation Shop to create animation.

Workshop

The workshop contains a question and answer section to help answer the most commonly asked questions and quiz questions to help you solidify your understanding of the material covered.

Q&A

Q Why do gradients look 3D?

A A gradient can give the appearance of depth because we perceive lighter colors as being closer and darker colors as being further away.

22

Q Can you use any shape for buttons?

A Absolutely! Some people may argue that a button should look like a button, but this is not the case. As long as people can identify the image as a button, you should be able to use any shape.

Q Is it worthwhile to use buttons from web libraries?

A It can be. Some libraries contain really good images. You may prefer to create your own, though, so that your web pages look original.

Quiz

1. Which tools in PSP do you use most often to create basic buttons?
2. How can gradients help you create more sophisticated buttons?
3. Why is tiling important when producing images for the web?
4. Which tool is primarily used to create a tiling effect?

Answers

1. The Shapes tool is a good starting point. You can use it to create the basic shapes you need for most buttons.
2. Gradients can give buttons a 3D quality.
3. When you create an image that can be tiled, only that small image is loaded. The browser takes care of tiling the image. Using a small image that tiles is preferable to using a large image because of the time involved in downloading large images.
4. The Clone Brush tool is often needed to cover up seams that appear during the process of creating an image that can tile seamlessly.

Hour **23**

Animation

Animation is one of the hottest topics on the web today. You can use Animation Shop alone or with Paint Shop Pro to create cool animations for your web pages.

Jasc's Animation Shop, which ships with Paint Shop Pro 5, is powerful yet easy to use. In this hour, I explain the following concepts:

- What animation is and how it works
- Why use animation
- Creating your first animation, including animated GIFs for your web pages
- Editing your first animation
- Using transitions
- Creating text effects

Animation Concepts

Whether it's an animated GIF for your web page or the latest box office blockbuster, all animations are basically the same.

The concept involves rapidly displaying a series of images, or frames, so that the human eye is fooled into seeing one long, continuous moving picture.

In movies, for example, each frame is captured on film and is then displayed on a screen, using a movie projector. Each frame is displayed for a very short time, followed by the next frame, and so on.

In animated GIFs, a digital artist uses computer software to create each frame. The frames are then displayed, using other software such as a web browser. Because each frame is displayed in succession and done so rapidly, the person viewing the animation sees one continuous movie.

Why Use Animation?

I have to tell you, I was one of the last people to jump on the animated GIF bandwagon. At first, I found the animations cheesy and poorly done. As the animations got better, and the software to create them more powerful, I changed my tune.

In the world of the web, many different elements are competing for your reader's attention. Even a single web page can offer dozens of images for your reader's eyes to wade through. This situation is the same on virtually every web page. If you want to run a banner ad, how do you attract a reader's attention? How do you get his or her eyes to see through all the other flashy, attractive graphics on the same web page?

One answer is animation. By animating an image, you make it stand out. You make it attract the reader's attention. Many of the ad banners you see at the top of web pages these days are animated.

Animation Shop enables you to animate your ads, buttons, and other graphical elements, too.

Building an Animation

Recall that an animation is a series of images or frames. You can create these frames in Paint Shop Pro or, to some extent, in Animation Shop.

You should be able to start Animation Shop by clicking the Start button at the bottom of the Windows 95 screen and choosing Programs, Paint Shop 5, Animation Shop.

Animation Shop's interface is simple and quite similar to Paint Shop Pro's (see Figure 23.1).

FIGURE 23.1.

*Animation Shop's
interface.*

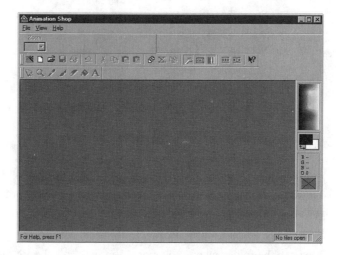

23

The tools are quite basic and of more use to touch up an animation than to create one. Creating an animation with both Paint Shop Pro and Animation Shop is quite easy, though, as the following exercise shows.

Creating Your First Animation

The best way to learn how to use Paint Shop Pro to create an animation is to dive right in. Try this exercise:

1. Start Paint Shop Pro.

2. Create a new 400×100, 72-pixel-per-inch image with the background color set to black and the image type set to 16.7 million colors.

3. Create a second image with the same settings.

4. Turn on the grid (View, Grid).

5. Select the Shapes tool (it resembles a small outlined square).

6. Under the Tool Controls tab in the Controls palette, set the shape to Circle and the style to Filled.

7. Set the foreground color to green and, in the first image, draw a circle near the left side. I used the grid, placed the mouse pointer at the center of the second vertical line, and drew a 55-pixel circle.

   I repeated this process with red and drew a circle in the second image at the center of the second-to-last vertical line (see Figure 23.2).

8. Save each image. I saved them both as PSP files in a temporary folder and called the first one green and the second one red (inventive, eh?).

FIGURE 23.2.

Two images containing colorful circles.

9. With the images safely saved on your hard drive, run Animation Shop.

10. Choose File, Open and open the Green.psp image. You should see the image appear on the screen.

11. Choose Edit, Insert Frames, From File.

12. Browse to the folder where you stored the files and choose the Red.psp file. Click OK. You'll now have two frames.

    You may see only one frame, but you can use the slider bar at the bottom of the image to scroll between both images (see Figure 23.3).

FIGURE 23.3.

Two-frame animation in Animation Shop.

Now you have all that's necessary for an animation. It might be a simple one, granted, but it is indeed an animation. To see your new movie, choose View, Animation.

When the flashing circles start to drive you crazy, close the animation by clicking on the small X in the upper-right corner of the window. That's it! You've created an animated GIF!

Of course, it was small, and it didn't do much. However, with a little tweaking, it could be pretty cool, as simple as it is. In fact, I have a similar animation running in the middle of an image on my web page. You can view the animation by entering the following URL into your web browser: `http://www.grafx-design.com/HireUs.html`.

On that page, you'll see a small interface with two blinking lights. The concept behind those lights is the same as the ones you've just created.

The lights I used are smaller (and a little less annoying). I also played around with adding frames with the lights turned off and both lights turned on, and I played with the interframe timing, as well.

Even as small as those lights are, they grab your attention. They're almost hypnotic (and that's the intent).

Editing Your First Animation

If you'd like to tweak the animation you just created, you can do so in Animation Shop. The first step is to create a blank, black rectangle to serve as a frame in which both lights are off. To do so, follow these steps:

1. From Animation Shop, choose Edit, Insert Frames, Empty.

2. For the moment, leave the defaults set in the Insert Empty Frames dialog box and click OK. You'll now have a new frame in your animation.

3. You can use the scroll bar at the bottom of the window to scroll to the frame. You'll see that it's empty—transparent, in fact.

4. You can fill it with black by setting the foreground color to black and using the Flood Fill tool to fill the entire frame with black.

5. You can view the new version of your animation by choosing View, Animation. Because of the speed with which your frames are being displayed, the extra frame is hard to see.

Now try this:

1. Stop the animation if it's still running.

2. Select the Arrow tool and use it to choose the all-black frame.

3. Choose Edit, Frame Properties.

4. Under the Display Time tab, enter **100** for the display time and click OK.

5. Run your animation again (View, Animation). Be sure to save this animation, because you will use it in the following sections.

Notice the difference? The lights flash, then there's a pause followed by the lights flashing, another pause, and so on.

You can edit this animation further by adding other black frames (adding blank frames) or changing the amount of time that a frame is displayed.

Using Transitions

Animation Shop has some built-in effects—called transitions—that can be used with your animations. *Transitions* are a way to move from one image to another. They are effects such as fading from one image to another.

To see how transitions work, follow these steps in Animation Shop:

1. Select the middle black frame with the Arrow tool and choose Edit, Delete to delete that frame. You'll be left with the first two frames: the green light and the red light.

2. To run a transition effect on the animation, choose Effects, Image Transitions. Doing so brings up the Add Image Transition dialog box (see Figure 23.4).

FIGURE 23.4.

The Add Image Transition dialog box.

3. Transition effects add an effect between frames or from one frame to an effect.

   With the two frames of the current animation and the Blinds effect, the animation goes from one frame, the green light, to the other frame, the red light, giving the effect of blinds opening and closing.

4. To see this effect, simply click OK and then choose View, Animation. Note how the image goes through a transition from one frame to the other.

You can add different effects, as well. You can apply a long list of built-in effects to your animation.

Try the Fade effect with the two lights. Much better than the annoying flashing created in the first exercise.

Play around with some of the effects, and I'm sure you'll get some ideas of the types of frames that you'd like to create to use the effects on. I think, for example, that the Spin effect would be a good way to treat some text.

Speaking of text, Animation Shop also enables you to create some text effects; they're discussed next.

23

Creating Text Effects

To create an animation using the built-in text effects, open a new file in Animation Shop (choose File, New) and choose Effects, Text Transitions. *Text transitions* are transformations involving text. You can, for example, get text to appear to wave in the wind.

In the Add Text Transition dialog box (see Figure 23.5), you can add text and choose an effect.

*The Add Text
Transition dialog box.*

Of course, you can create your own text animations, using Paint Shop Pro to create the text frames and then importing the frames into Animation Shop. You might want to play around with some of the built-in effects to see what's possible, though.

Certainly, if you want truly spectacular results, you'll want to create your frames in Paint Shop Pro. You can actually create a multilayered image in Paint Shop Pro and use the layers as frames for an animation. This technique enables you to create the best animations for your web pages, as you'll see in the next hour.

Summary

This hour introduced GIF animation and Animation Shop. I showed you how to create a simple two-frame animation, how to insert a frame, and how to change the timing of the frames. I also showed you how to apply some of the built-in effects that come with Animation Shop.

In the next, and final, hour, I walk you through the process of using Paint Shop Pro and Animation Shop to create a more complex animation.

Workshop

The workshop contains a question and answer section to help answer the most commonly asked questions and quiz questions to help you solidify your understanding of the material covered.

Q&A

Q How do I use layers as frames?

A That option is covered in the next hour.

Q Can I drag images directly from Paint Shop Pro to Animation Shop?

A No. You need to save your images from Paint Shop Pro and then open them in Animation Shop.

Q If I place a frame in the wrong place, can I quickly move it to the right location?

A Yes. You can also cut and paste, or copy and paste, frames.

Quiz

1. What is an animation? Why can an animation help make your web page a better place to visit?

2. What is a transition? What program do you use to add transitions to your animations?

3. What is an animated GIF?

Answers

1. An animation is an image that contains a series of frames that, when repeated, gives the illusion of movement. Animations can add to the quality of a web site in the same way that good images can.

2. A transition is a transformation that takes place between one image and another. These are usually effects such as fading. You can use Animation Shop's built-in transformations, or you can use various effects in Paint Shop Pro to create your own.

3. An animated GIF is a GIF file that contains several frames that can be played in an image viewer or web browser. As these frames are displayed, they give the illusion of movement much the same as motion pictures do.

23

HOUR 24

Advanced Animation

The best way to create an animation is to create a layered image in Paint
Shop Pro and open the .PSP file as a multiframed animation in Animation
Shop. With the file saved as a .PSP file, you can go back and make any
changes, add new layers, rearrange the layers, and so on.

These two programs form a powerful combination for creating animated
GIFs for your web pages. I cover the following more-advanced animation
topics in this hour:

- Using layered images and masks in animation
- Creating a spinning globe animation
- Understanding advanced animation techniques

Using Layers and Masks in Animation

Using Paint Shop Pro and Animation Shop together enables you to create
amazingly complex animations.

You can create an image in Paint Shop Pro, using layers, masks, and any of the effects you'd like. Then you can import the resulting file into Animation Shop as a multiframed animation.

The following section shows you how to build a spinning globe animation.

Putting Your Own Spin on the World

You'll need to find an image of the world that has been flattened. Many clip art sites and CD-ROMs have maps of the world and globes, so you should be able to find one similar to the one I'm using.

If you're handy with the Paint Brushes tools, you might even create your own. Figure 24.1 shows the image I'm using.

FIGURE 24.1.

The (pre-Columbus) world.

This map shows the world flattened out. Actually, the map shows two copies of the world so that you can wrap the entire image around a sphere and not miss any parts or have any unruly seams.

The image I'm using is 630×150. To leave some space around the edges of the new image that I'll create, I open a new 200×200 image. What I'll be doing is cutting and pasting 150×150 portions of the flattened globe into different layers of the new image. Follow these steps:

1. Open a new 200×200 image.
2. In the Background layer, create a centered blue circle that's 150 pixels in radius (see Figure 24.2).

FIGURE 24.2.

This circle will become the oceans.

3. Make copies of the blue circle for each layer that you will be pasting a portion of the globe onto.

   You can make the copy by clicking-and-dragging the Background layer onto the Add New Layer icon each time you want to create a new layer.

4. Then copy and paste a portion of the globe to a new image, resize the canvas to 150×150, and apply the Circle Deformation filter (choose Image, Deformations, Circle) to the new image. This deformed portion of the globe will be copied again and pasted onto the new blue circle layer.

5. Repeat this process until you've copied the entire globe into new layers of the new file.

I'll walk through creating the first few layers:

1. I've opened the World image and created a new 200×200 image (see Figure 24.3).

2. To start, select the Selection tool and set the selection type to Square, the Feather value to 0, and turn off anti-aliasing.

3. Place the mouse pointer at 0, 0 in the World image and make a 150×150 pixel selection.

4. Choose Edit, Copy to copy the selection to the Clipboard.

FIGURE 24.3.

Both the World and the Ocean files in Paint Shop Pro.

24

5. Then choose Edit, Paste, As New Image.

6. Expand the image size with Image, Resize, because only the portion of the image that has information gets pasted.

   Therefore, because of the transparent background, the image comes in smaller than 150×150.

7. To resize the new image, choose Image, Canvas Size and enter **150** for both the New Width and New Height.

8. To make a sphere of the new area that you've copied from the flattened world, apply the Circle deformation with Image, Deformations, Circle.

   Doing so wraps the image around a sphere, giving it back its shape (remember that you are using a flattened image of Earth).

9. Choose Selections, Select All and Edit, Copy to copy this portion of the world to the Clipboard.

10. Add a layer to the Globe image (the one that you created and added a blue ball—er, oceans—to) by clicking-and-dragging the Background layer onto the Add New Layer icon.

11. Name this layer World01 by double-clicking the layer in the Layers palette and giving the layer a name in the dialog box that appears.

12. Paste the portion of the world you just created directly onto this layer by choosing Edit, Paste, As New Selection.

That's how each layer is created.

To create the second layer, follow these steps:

1. Start the selection on the World image at 20, 0 (for each new layer, move 20 pixels to the right) and copy and paste this selection.

2. Resize and deform it and then select it and paste it onto a new blue circle.

Create each new layer the same way until you have 15 world layers. You'll need all 15 to get the entire globe into the animation.

Saving and Optimizing Files in Animation Shop

To save the image so that it can be opened in Animation Shop, I turned on all the layers except the Background layer. (I turned off most of them as I created each layer to avoid confusion.)

Animation Shop adds each visible layer as a frame when it opens a .PSP file.

With the file saved, it's time to open it in Animation Shop. Before doing so, though, you must change the preferences in Animation Shop. In Animation Shop, choose File, Preferences, General Program Preferences and click on the Layered Files tab (see Figure 24.4).

FIGURE 24.4.

Setting the Layered Files preferences in Animation Shop.

24

Place a checkmark in the Keep Each Layer as a Separate Frame checkbox. This feature makes Animation Shop open a multilayered file and keep each layer as a separate frame. It's a very powerful feature.

With the preferences set up properly, it's time to open the image. Choose File, Open and browse to the file you saved in Paint Shop Pro. In my case, it's the Spin file (the final image I saved in Paint Shop Pro).

To view the animation, choose View, Animation. If the image checks out, you can save it as a web-ready animated GIF.

Before saving the file, you should optimize it. To do so, choose File, Optimization Wizard. This step opens the Optimized Output dialog box (see Figure 24.5).

FIGURE 24.5.

Animation Shop's Optimized Output dialog box.

Place a checkmark in the Animated GIF File and the Create a New Animation from the Optimized Animation checkboxes. Click Next. Then choose the Optimization setting you want (see Figure 24.6).

FIGURE 24.6.

Animation Shop's Animation Quality Versus Output Size dialog box.

Most times, you'll want the maximum compression to keep your file sizes small for the web.

You'll have to judge how the settings affect the image quality, though. Sometimes making an image as small as possible is not the way to go. If you find that the quality of the final image suffers, you might want to sacrifice a little size for some quality.

You'll see a dialog box with several progress charts, and then you'll see the final optimization dialog box, which shows you the savings you get from the optimization (see Figure 24.7).

FIGURE 24.7.

Animation Shop's Optimization Results dialog box.

This final dialog box shows you how much space is saved, the optimized file size, and the time it will take to download at various modem speeds. On my 56Kbps modem, the spinning globe takes eight seconds to download.

The nice thing about working with Paint Shop Pro and Animation Shop together is that if, for example, I find this file to be too large, I can simply resize the file in Paint Shop Pro, resave it, and open it again in Animation Shop.

Spreading Your Wings

If you'd like to practice some of the techniques I've described in this hour, you can open the bttrfly.psp file that comes with Paint Shop Pro.

You can open it in Paint Shop Pro and examine each layer; you can open the file in Animation Shop as well to see how the final animation turned out.

I suggest you create a few animations using images created in Paint Shop Pro. Start with a few layers and see how the process works; then attack a more ambitious project. Remember to have some fun and try different things as you work with both of these amazing programs.

Summary

In this hour, I showed you how to create a multiframe animation from a multilayered Paint Shop Pro file. I also introduced you to the optimization process. I encourage you to build a few animations and experiment with both Animation Shop and Paint Shop Pro.

I hope you enjoyed this book and that you have as much fun reading it as I did writing it. See you on the web (virtually speaking, of course).

—T. Michael Clark

Workshop

The workshop contains a question and answer section to help answer the most commonly asked questions and quiz questions to help you solidify your understanding of the material covered.

Q&A

Q Can you drag files from Paint Shop Pro into Animation Shop?

A Nope. That might be one feature that the engineers at Jasc Software would consider adding, though.

Q Is there a limit to the number of layers you can have?

A Although I imagine there must be some sort of limit, I have not yet encountered it. I doubt that, in the course of creating images and animation frames, you'll ever come across a limit, either.

Q Can I animate JPG images?

A Good question, and one I've seen and responded to before. Unfortunately, the answer is no. It's the properties of the GIF file that enable it to hold the various frames that make up an animation. I suppose you could, if you wanted to, write a Java program that would constantly replace JPG images over each other. Although this technique might work, it wouldn't really be practical. Animated GIFs are fairly compact, will run on virtually any browser, and require no programming.

Q Can I load JPG images into Animation Shop?

A Although the final animation will be a GIF file, you certainly can build it from JPG files.

Quiz

1. How do you properly save a Paint Shop Pro image with multiple layers into Animation Shop?

2. How are masks and layers imported into Animation Shop from Paint Shop Pro to make them animations?

3. What does Animation Shop do to each visible Paint Shop Pro layer in its own format?

4. Where do you set the Animation Shop preferences for importing and exporting files?

5. What is optimization? How does it help you?

Answers

1. You have to first turn on all the layers you want to import because Animation Shop adds each visible layer as a frame. Then you simply save the image as a PSP file. The resulting file can then be opened as a multiframe file in Animation Shop.

2. Masks aren't imported, but the effect they have on a layer will still be evident in the animated image. Every layer is imported as a separate frame in the animation.

3. Each visible layer in a PSP file is converted into a frame in Animation Shop.

4. In the General Program Preferences dialog box, click on the Layered Files tab and place a checkmark in the Keep Each Layer as a Separate Frame option.

5. There are different types of optimization. Essentially, each type tries to minimize the final file size while maintaining the quality of the image.

APPENDIX **A**

Paint Shop Pro Resources

For more information on Paint Shop Pro, you can try three basic areas: the web, Usenet, and other published material.

Try these Paint Shop Pro tutorial web sites:

- GrafX Design at `http://www.grafx-design.com`
- Jasc Software Inc. at `http://www.jasc.com`
- i/us at `http://www.i-us.com`
- Cheap Tricks at `http://www.iland.net/~delevan`
- Sumrall Works at `http://www.sumrallworks.com`
- Predator Graphics at `http://members.aol.com/grfxdezign`
- Wagoner PSP Tutorials Unlimited at
  `http://www.kconline.com/fwagoner/indexpsptu.htm`

Many of the preceding sites also contain links to other Paint Shop Pro tutorial web sites, so if you don't find what you want right away, keep digging.

Try these Usenet sites:

- `comp.graphics.apps.paint-shop-pro`
- `comp.graphics`
- `comp.graphics.misc`
- `alt.graphics`
- `comp.infosystems.web.authoring.images`

Software companies on the web include the following:

- Jasc Software at `http://www.jasc.com`
- Auto F/X at `http://autofx.com`
- Alien Skin at `http://www.alienskin.com`
- Metacreations at `http://www.metacreations.com`
- Corel at `http://www.corel.com`
- Adobe at `http://www.adobe.com`
- RAYflect at `http://www.rayflect.com`
- Flaming Pear at `http://www.ccn.cs.dal.ca/~aa731/blade.html`
- Xara at `http://www.xara.com`

Finally, you can read my other book, *Paint Shop Pro Web Techniques,* published in 1997 by New Riders (ISBN: 1-56205-756-1). It includes a lot more web-specific techniques and examples and, although the book was written for version 4.0, most of the techniques work in version 5.0.

INDEX

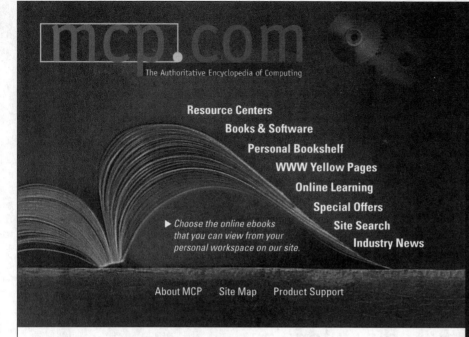